Calling Dr. Laura

Also by Nicole Georges:

INVINCIBLE SUMMER

A Mariner Original
Mariner Books
Houghton Mifflin Harcourt
Boston New York

The names of some humans in this book have been changed. The author has tried to remain as truthful as possible, but has taken the liberty of melting together certain individuals in order to protect the innocent and not bore readers.

www.hmhco.com

Library of Congress Cataloging-in-Publication Data
Georges, Nicole J.
Calling Dr. Laura : a graphic memoir / Nicole J. Georges.
p. cm. -- (Mariner books)
ISBN 978-0-547-61559-2
1. Georges, Nicole J. -- Comic books, strips, etc. 2. Schlessinger, Laura. -- Comic books, strips, etc. 3. Identity (Psychology) -- Comic books, strips, etc. 4. Family secrets -- Comic books, strips, etc. 5. Graphic novels. I. Title. II. Title: Calling Doctor Laura.
PN6727.G466C35 2013
741.5'973 -- dc23
[B]
2012022389

Printed in China
SCP 10 9 8 7 6 5 4 3

Production assistance by Harlan Mahaffy.

For my sisters

Chocolate peanut butter cups were a really popular item during this time, as they were the only fail-proof recipe in the vegan cookbook my Portland friends all owned.

The book was from Canada, & had somehow gone awry in the conversion from metric. As a result, "cookie bars" were hockey pucks, & brownies like biscuits.

The peanut butter cups were a stroke of luck, delicious + unscathed.

I DIDN'T TELL HER THAT CHOCOLATE PEANUT BUTTER CUPS TAKE AN HOUR TO SET (IN THE FRIDGE) BEFORE YOU EAT THEM, BUT I DID MENTION THE DREAM.

It was really romantic!

Does your person have a moustache?
no.

Anne
Peter
Eric
Does your person look like Rodney Dangerfield?
No

hmmm.
snap
snap
snap

We should check the peanut butter cups, right?

!!!

WE ATE THE PEANUT BUTTER CUPS AT THEIR APPROPRIATELY CHILLED TIME.

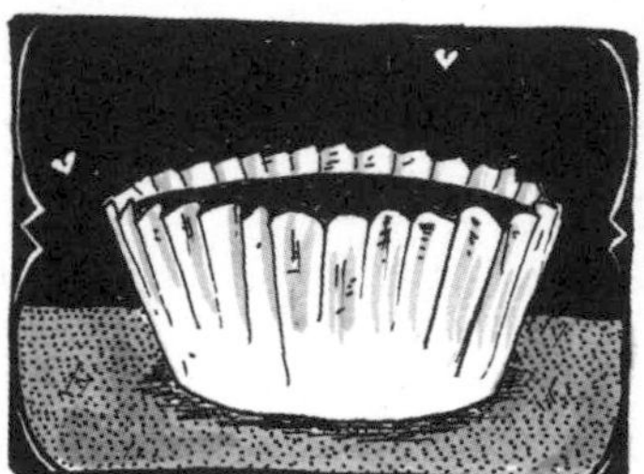

My trick worked! I lured a girl into my room & had a magical time while we waited for baked goods to cool.

Therein lay our problem –
I DID WANT A GIRLFRIEND.

I FELT READY, AFTER YEARS OF CHAOS, FOR SOMETHING STABLE. SOMETHING I COULD INVEST IN.

(WE CAN DISCUSS THE CHAOS LATER.)

I WAS ONLY 22 WHEN I KISSED VERONA MAUSS, BUT I WAS ALREADY TIRED OF MY TOWN'S NONCOMMITTAL DATING POPULATION. THE DISCOVERY THAT SHE WAS AMONG THEM MADE MY JOINTS ACHE. PREMATURELY GERIATRIC & SEEKING SHELTER, I KEPT LOOKING.

I KEPT LOOKING, BUT WE REMAINED FRIENDS. WE COULDN'T DATE, PER SE, BUT WE DRANK MILK-SHAKES IN MY HAMMOCK + TOLD STORIES WHILE SPOONING.

IS IT T.M.I. TO TELL YOU THAT THERE WAS ALWAYS SOME TENSION? SEXUAL RESIDUE LEFT OVER FROM OUR EARLIEST DAYS. THIS WAS RARELY REALIZED, ONLY NOTED.

that is Verona in a nutshell...
I'D FIGHT A GANG FOR HER, AND IN TURN SHE'D "KILL SOMEONE, DRESS THEM AS A GIANT CRICKET, AND FEED THEM TO A LIZARD" FOR ME.
A true blue friend.
ONE FEBRUARY DAY SHE DELIVERED MY BIRTHDAY PRESENT.
We have to drive there.
where?
It's top secret.
THIS PRESENT WAS TWO MONTHS BELATED, AS WE HAD TO SET IT UP LIKE AN APPOINTMENT.
(IT WAS HARD TO FIND TIME AROUND MY BIRTHDAY, WHEN I TRADITIONALLY RETURN HOME TO KANSAS.)
SOMETHING I FORGOT TO MENTION ABOUT VERONA:
SHE DOES NOT DRIVE.
Let's go.
And so it was that she led me to my mysterious birthday appointment from the passenger seat of my new orange car...
Turn right here. ...Wait, no...yeah, left here.

WE WALKED UP TRENDY HAWTHORNE STREET AND STOPPED BEFORE A LARGE, NONDESCRIPT HOUSE.

WE KNOCKED. WAITED.
THE WOMAN WHO ANSWERED THE DOOR LOOKED KIND OF LIKE ONE OF MY MOM'S CHURCH FRIENDS, COMPLETE WITH CRUCIFIX. STILL CONFUSED, I TRIED TO BE POLITE.
Come in. You're late.
Have a seat. I'm almost ready for you.
Thanks!
It's for her birthday.
Really? Happy birthday. You can go first.
Oh... thanks! It was a couple months ago, but ... thanks!

I got you A palM reading for your birthday.
?
NO way!!!
How did you find A palm reader????
I found her in the back of the newspaper.

friend
forever
I didnt tell Verona everything that happened at my palm reading.
PALMIST
EXPERIENCED
$30/SESSION
503-555-5555
You will meet a man your senior this summer.
I TOLD VERONA ABOUT MY LOVE PREDICTIONS,
You will have three pregnancies...
...but only two children.
And MY FUTURE KIDS...
But I DID NOT TELL HER WHAT OCCURED DURING THE FIRST FIVE MINUTES OF MY SESSION.
Sit down.
Have you ever had a palm reading before?
no.
Well nothing said today is personal,
and please keep it to yourself for at least 24 hours.

Why did she say that?... Can she psychically tell that I'm a gossip?
Oh.
It looks like you have conflicts with your mother?
yes-
Oh. Actually my father's dead.
and you really should talk to your father more often.
Maybe the man you think is your father is dead...
... but your real father is very much alive.

uh...
Hmm.
Now...
Who is this bitch?
Who does she think she is?
You'll live a long, healthy life.
Of course he's dead.
...Of course he is.
so then...

She INSISTED I was on DRUGS!
She said she could tell I was into something "dark."
Just because you're wearing black, I'm sure.
Did you tell her you were gay?
...No. did you?
No.
Did she tell you about your Soul Mate?
Yeah. I'M Going to marry a rich man.
Me too!
I KEPT THE PART ABOUT MY FAMILY TO MYSELF FOR TWENTY-FOUR HOURS.

Z Z Z Z Z Z Z
...AND THEN I KEPT THE PART ABOUT MY FAMILY TO MYSELF FOR ALMOST A YEAR.

For as long as I can remember, I have felt adopted.

MY SISTERS AND I HAVE TWO SETS OF FATHERS, SO THERE WAS NO ONE IN THE FAMILY WITH WHOM I OBSERVED OR FELT A STRONG GENETIC BOND.

THEY BOTH LOOK LIKE MY MOM.

Look at our Syrian noses!

?

I just can't believe y'all look so much alike!

I know Nicole, it's because we're re-late-d.

AS I RESEMBLE NO ONE, I HAVE ALWAYS BEEN IN AWE OF SIMILAR SIBLINGS.

Note: MY MOM IS REFERENCING A PHOTO OF HER GRANDMOTHER AT AGE 90. SHRUNKEN & ROTUND.

THE ONLY FLAW IN MY ADOPTION THEORY IS THAT MY MOTHER WAS IN NO WAY FIT TO ADOPT A CHILD IN 1980.
SHE WAS A WORKING MOM IN D.C., STRUGGLING TO SUPPORT TWO TEENAGED DAUGHTERS.
(Who had similar features as they were related to one another.)
Not TO MENTION MY MOM'S FAVORITE PART OF RETELLING MY LIFE STORY:
SO, I went to the hospital in labor, nine months pregnant.
whoo whoo whoo
ADMITTANCE
and the intake form says
How did you get into this Condition?
ADMITTANCE
so I say...
One Fine night in Ensenada
!
ADMITTANCE

after a couple Margaritas...
ewww. Mommm!
What?!? It's the truth!
You were my unexpected love child!
AAAACK!
So, with that haunting my imagination, I've always had a pretty good idea that she was at least somewhat involved in my conception.
She even had an ultrasound with matching story.
"OSCAR"
We called you Oscar before you were born, Nick. We thought you were a boy!
The week before you were born, I had a dream.
- A premonition.
!!!
In it, I was passed out on the table & Doctors were running around.
I saw blood and surgeon's tools, but no baby.

So when I went into labor, I said "No Drugs" because I thought I'd lose you.
AAARRGH!
It was terrible! You were such a pain, you got all flipped over with the cord wrapped around your neck!
They had to reach inside of me & flip-
eww, Mom!
I'm done having kids!
Anyway, the labor was so hard that I had them go ahead and tie my tubes while I was in there.
And I had a stroke right there on the operating table.
It was JUST LIKE IN MY DREAM! Your Mother's very psychic, Nickie.

* SQUEE-GEE = AFFECTIONATE NICKNAME BASED ON MY CHUB & SQUEEZABILITY AS A BABY.

The Dead Dads Club

I HAD A LOT OF FATHERLESS FRIENDS THROUGH MY ADOLESCENCE & TEEN YEARS.

TO BE SPECIFIC, I HAD SEVERAL FRIENDS WHOSE FATHERS HAD PASSED AWAY.

INFORMALLY, THIS WAS CALLED THE DEAD DADS CLUB AND CONSISTED OF WHOMEVER I COULD FIND.

FOR MOST OF US, THE LOSS HAD HAPPENED IN THE DISTANT PAST, AND WE'D HARDENED TO THE POINT OF IT BEING A DARK JOKE.

!!!
Hey, MOM, guess what!? Rachel's dad is dead too & she gets Social Security checks each month!
We should apply for that!
Well, um, I think it's too late. We would've had to apply for that a while ago.
?
Oh...
rats!
Snap
Oh well.
Hey, Tom! Let's go get chocolate cokes!
I MOVED ON EASILY, JUST HAPPY TO FIT IN WITH MY FELLOW SEMI-ORPHANS.

Portland

KILLINGSWORTH ST.
GEORGES
ORTH
Georges
sports bar
Gustav's
2268

sniff
Beija, Quit.
Needles are too sharp for you.
BRRRRING
... hello?
mmm hmm
A stray?
Yeah, I could pick her up right now.
I need a box!
Got to go, Beija.

You stay here and guard the house.
I'll be back.
GEORGE

We found her walking down the street.
No one claimed her, so...
Thanks! I'm so excited to take her home!
thank you.
No, thank you! Really, I didn't know what to do with a stray chicken!
Hey!
What you got there?!
A chicken!
You gonna eat it?
what's she got?
No way! It's a pet, not a dinner!

A pet!?!
!!!
ha
ha
ha
ha
Well have fun, then!
I will!
Bye!
You don't even need to lay eggs for me. I do not eat them.
bwaaa?
Olde Tyme Sewing Co.
Nope. You can just hang out in the yard and
chill with the other chicken ladies.

Who are you?
bwaa?
Mavis?
Margaret?
...Mabel?
bwaa?
you are Mabel.
Beija, - stay -
bwaaa
bwa bwa!

Bwaaaa
Cluck!

EDMONDO WAS A GIFT FROM 40 YEAR OLD ED TO FOUR YEAR OLD ME ON HIS FIRST DATE WITH MY MOTHER.

THIS IS HOW MY CHILDHOOD TOY, THE LONE SURVIVOR OF YOUTH TO JOIN ME IN BED EACH NIGHT AS AN ADULT, WOULD BEAR (!) THE SAME NAME AS MY SOON-TO-BE STEPFATHER, ED.

Man, I was so slender there! I was a size 6 in these photos... ...And tan!
sigh.
mom..
WE MOVED TO FLORIDA FOR ED'S JOB, AND WHILE OUR TANS WERE CAUSED BY NATURAL SUNSHINE, HER SIZE WAS SUCH FROM A STEADY DIET OF CIGARETTES, STRESS, & ABUSE.

$#!*
I CAN'T RECALL THERE EVER BEING PEACEFUL MIDDLE GROUND IN FLORIDA, ONLY CONFLICT.

I ASKED MOM ONCE WHY SHE MARRIED ED. WITH NO TRACE OF ROMANTICISM, SHE REPLIED "I JUST WANTED A DAD FOR YOU."

Why are you covering your ears, Mondy?
Because they're too loud and they're scaring me.
SLAP!
thud
my pet monster (TM)
... BUT THAT'S A STORY FOR ANOTHER DAY.

Don't worry, Edmondo, I'll take care of you.
I'm right here with you.
sigh

Paragon
LIVE
KARA
NO MINORS
PERMITTED
ON PREMISES

Paragon
LIVE KARAOKE
NO MINORS PERMITTED

Paragon
LIVE KARAOKE
NO MINORS PERMITTED

Paragon

Paragon
LIVE KARAO
At THE PARAGON, YOU HAD TO GET BUZZED IN. PRESS A BUTTON & MAKE EYE CONTACT WITH THE BARTENDER FOR ENTRY.

THE DOORS WERE COVERED IN THICK GRATES TO DISCOURAGE DRUG DEALERS.
ONE TIME A LADY GOT STABBED DURING KARAOKE.
I Got stABBED!
IT HAPPENED IN THE BATHROOM, LIKE DURING A FIGHT.
TIPS
NO PLAYLIST
·I LIKE BIG BUTTS
·KILLING ME SOFTLY
·STRO
RULES:
NO YELLING
NO WHINING
NO CURSING INTO THE MIC!
cLick
BY TITLE
STABBING LIKE THIS.
!
NOT LIKE THIS.
so I wasn't too concerned

I got a job

AT THE PARAGON AFTER MY FRIEND LISA STARTED A RIOT, CAUSING THE OLD KARAOKE JOCKEY TO QUIT.

THE REGULAR K.J. WAS GONE, AND IN HER PLACE WAS A SOUR-FACED GUY WHO DECLARED:

First of All:

HOW CAN YOU SAY SUCH A THING???

and

Secondly:

WE MET UP AT THE PARAGON SPECIFICALLY FOR A NIRVANA TRIBUTE NIGHT, AND NOW FOUND OURSELVES DERAILED BY THIS WICKED MAN.

ONCE THE K.J. STARTED VISIBLY THROWING OUT OUR SONG REQUESTS, LISA TOOK A STAND.

HE TURNED LISA'S MICROPHONE OFF AS SHE SANG THE BIG BOPPER.

SHE WAS READY. SHE TURNED ON HIM.

(so drunk)
She knocked off his hat, threw his glasses, and scattered song slips, tips, and books everywhere.
TIPS
As a person with glasses, I recognized this as a major dis.
I QUIT!
Lisa ran out before the police arrived.
I figured they'd need a new karaoke jockey.
Paragon
LIV
KARA
I applied the next morning
NO IN/ OUT PRIVILEGES

We put the pig in the ground, we got the beer on ice
NO PLAY LIST
· I LIKE BIG BUTTS
· KILLING ME SOFTLY
· STROKIN'
MY RULES
NO YELLING
NO WHINING
NO CURSING into the Mic!
ALL MY ROWDY FRIENDS
OVER TONIGGHHt
CLAP CLAP CLAP CLAP CLAP CLAP
WAHOO!
thank you, Casey!
NO PLAY LIST
· I LIKE BIG BUTTS
MY. RULES
NO YELLING
NO WHINING
NO CURSING INTO THE MIC!
Next up we have ... ... Kate!

VERONA FAITHFULLY KEPT ME COMPANY AT KARAOKE EVERY WEEK.

SHE USED TO LIKE MOOCHING OFF MY FREE DRINKS.

TONIGHT SOMETHING WAS DIFFERENT.

A round of applause for Kate!

Her NAME WAS RADAR, AND SHE SHOWED UP WITH MY NEIGHBOR MONA.

Oooh AAAH Ooh AAAH Why Do Fools Fall in Love
I'D MET RADAR EARLIER IN THE DAY, AT MONA'S HOUSE.
Here. It's a flier for my karaoke night.
hi, Nicole
Hi.
I'm already coming.
Good! Take this anyway!
I HEARD SHE WAS VISITING PORTLAND TO HEAL FROM A DIVORCE.
AND LOVERS AWAIT THE BREAK OF DAY, WHY DO
Should I sing Jolene?
Who's next?
uh.... Valerie.
NO PLAY LIST
I LIKE BIG BUTTS
KILLING ME SOFTLY
STROKIN'
MY RULES
NO YELLING
NO WHINING
OKAYYYY... VALERIE! You're up!
WHEN I CAUGHT HER STARING AT THE K.J. BOOTH, I FIGURED SHE WAS SAD & STARING INTO SPACE, NOT LOOKING AT ME.
?
Hey.
SHE SURPRISED ME BY APPROACHING THE BOOTH WITH A PROPOSAL.

If you would have TOLD ME THAT RADAR JARONE WOULD BE THE ONE TO HELP ME UNRAVEL THE FAMILY SECRET, & TO CONFESS ONE OF MY OWN, I WOULD HAVE CALLED YOU CRAZY.
Like a
the sky I cry because you are my
Would you ever consider doing this somewhere else?
Like my family's tavern?
keep bumpin' heads I know that one of these days We gonna work it out
Oh! Umm... sure, Maybe.
You know, someone just got stabbed here last week, so that would probably be fun.
Actually, it wasn't that bad, it seemed more like a fight than a 'Stabbing', per se, but I actually had the week
Here. Email me.
so...
oh.
let this go you can't tell nobody
see ya.
CLAP CLAP CLAP CLAP
?
And that's it.
THE WHEELS WERE IN MOTION. THE PLAY HAD BEGUN, AND WITH THIS INTRODUCTION, ITS CONCLUSION FOREVER CHANGED.
LAST CALL, EVERYBODY!

MY STOMACH PAINS STARTED AROUND THE TIME MOM & ED GOT TOGETHER.

I DIDN'T WANT TO GO TO THE BATHROOM. I JUST DIDN'T.

SITTING DOWN, WAITING OUT THE URGE, WAS MY USUAL STATE OF AFFAIRS.

I WOULD GO TO GREAT LENGTHS TO AVOID THE TOILET.

It was important to wait until the feeling passed before standing up or moving around.

with Rapunzel hair, a-growin' down
A shimmy in a-strut
and a mane you never cut, make it all go 'round!
Ha!
Nothin' can compare to a girl's long hair
to make you act so silly
Make you sell your filly
Make you stick it all out
Then you jump and shout...
Oh Baby that's A-What I Like!
clap
clap
clap
Because if I didn't wait and control my urge to go...

Okay, girls, time to go home.
gulp
...my bowels couldn't control themselves.
Umm... can I wear this home and bring it back to you?
No. Why?
No Reason.
Come on, Nickie, let's go.
I'll just go change.
Oh no.

THE PRIZED TUTU.
I'D RUINED IT.
ewww!
What is it, Sweetie?
My OWN CLOTHES DIDN'T MATTER, BUT MESSING UP SOMEONE ELSE'S GARMENT?
Nickie ruined my tutu!
Gross!
What's the matter with her???
Don't talk to her anymore.
I won't. She's disgusting!
KNOCK
KNOCK

Knock Knock
Almost finished!
What're you doing in there?
Nothing!
Be Right There!

Ready to go?
yeah!
Where's the
Hey, did you know that
blah blah blah blah blah blah blah blah blah blah
tutu?
Oh wow, Nickie, that's great.
?
I know! Thank you!

I tried to EMAIL RADAR AFTER OUR MEETING AT THE PARAGON
MAIL
INBOX
JUNK
DRAFTS
SENT
DELETED
FROM:) NICOLEG.
TO:) RADARVD@GMALE.COM
SUBJECT:) KARAOKE
Hi Radar,
. . .
start
MAIL:
INBOX
JUNK
DRAFTS
SENT
DELETED
FROM:) NicoleG@Meowface.com
TO:) RADARVK@MAILFACE.COM
SUBJECT:) karaoke
Dear Radar,
FROM:) NicoleG@Meowface.com
TO:) RADARVK@MAILMAIL.COM
SUBJECT:) karaoke at
R,
Hi. It's Nicole...
BUT I WAS SUDDENLY SPEECHLESS, UNABLE TO FIND ONE PIECE OF SMALL TALK TO FILL IN THE NERVOUS SPACE IN MY BLANK LETTER.

SOMEHOW I DID IT, STARTED A CORRESPONDENCE.
hi... how... ..are.. ..you,.?
err..

AND NOW SHE WAS WALKING ACROSS THE STREET TO MEET ME, A PENPAL.

A REALLY FRIENDLY, VISITING PENPAL.

A REALLY FRIENDLY, CHIVALROUS, VISITING PENPAL.

PLEASE SEAT YOURSELF
THE EMAILS NEVER LED ME TO BELIEVE WE HAD A SPARK;

BUT HERE IT WAS, TOO AWKWARD TO BE ANYTHING BUT A DATE.
so, um... I hear you have four dogs?

L.A.'s just really different...
I wish you could see it.
...You know, to see that it's real.
Hey-
it's not like that.
oh!
Do you want to see something?
sure!

This is where you're staying?
Yep.
This is my Grandparents' house.
BOWL
They like to entertain.
Wow! It's...
Are you cold?
No.
SHE BUILT US A FIRE.
Those are some pretty serious tattoos.
yeah.
(SHE TURNED ON THE ELECTRIC FIREPLACE.)

I got it when I was 18...
yep.
...
My nerves were getting the best of me...
This one's from when I was 16.
Oh!
I was dating a cosmologist.
a.. what?
It's like, a psychic. A professional astrologer.
And I betrayed my personality by coming across as quiet and demure. Easygoing, even.
hmmm!

Hmm!
gulp
Oh!
I went to a palm reader for the first time this year.
JUST TO BREAK THE SILENCE.
Oh yeah?
So my friend says, "I got you an appointment some-where for your birthday."
I HADN'T TOLD ANYONE IN MY LIFE ABOUT THE DAD PREDICTION. ONLY RECENTLY HAD IT BEEN VOICED AT ALL (IN THERAPY), AND SO TELLING HER WAS LIKE PRACTICE.

Seeing HOW IT FELT IN THE AIR.
...and she told me this really crazy thing...
It GAVE US SOMETHING TO TALK ABOUT.
That's a really crazy story, Nicole.
yep.
Sometimes IT FEELS MUCH EASIER TO BARE INTENSELY PERSONAL INFORMATION WITH A STRANGER THAN TO TELL YOUR REAL FRIENDS.
umm...
I was like, "Who is this bitch?!?"
ha ha ha
It's LIKE SKIPPING THE BASES OF SMALL TALK AND STEALING HOME.
YOU DON'T HAVE TO BE EMOTIONALLY ACCOUNTABLE, BECAUSE THEY DON'T KNOW YOU.

You TELL THE STORY TWO STEPS AWAY. ALMOST OBJECTIVELY.
LIKE YOU SAW IT ON T.V., THAT FAR REMOVED.
And then
...So, you've asked your sisters what happened, right?
.....no.
You haven't?
no.
I'm afraid of what will happen.
I WASN'T READY YET.

I didn't tell you this part about the stomach pains...
ENCOPRESIS, from the Greek κοπρος (kopros; dung) is repeated, involuntary or inappropriate soiling in children older than 4 years.
ex. 1
There are both emotional and physical causes associated with Encopresis. The most common is constipation.
ex. 2
"When children experience constant constipation, the stool can become large, hard and dry. It creates a lot of pain that causes young children to avoid going to the toilet, creating more pain and difficulties."
"Over time, if the colon (large intestine) and rectum become stretched, the muscles and nerves will not signal the need to have a bowel movement. This leads to stool accidents."
-Huxley, Ron. "Childhood Encopresis: Causes and Treatment" (2008)
Emotional stress may also trigger Encopresis.

If I didn't know you'd been living this way for so long, I'd be alarmed.
The American Academy of Pediatrics states that "Fecal soiling can occur when a child is anxious or emotionally distraught over some aspect of his life over which he has little control such as family conflicts, academic difficulties, or problems with social relationships."
Lazy sphincter muscle?
MARCH
If you go, I'll give you this puppy, Nick!
I'm trying. I just can't.
Is it because it hurts?
Kind of?
Conventional treatments for physical symptoms (including diet, exercise, & incentives for toilet time) may offer short term relief but will not be ultimately successful if the emotional root has not been treated.

Encopredic children who have experienced trauma can greatly benefit from family therapy.
"They will need a caring, tolerant professional who can address the emotional issues underlying the disorder." - Huxley, 2008
Do you need to go freshen up?
Well, another cleaning lady quit. She found your bucket under the sink.
Sigh
What are you going to do when you want to start dating, Nick? When you want to be intimate with a man?
blech.
NO ENCOPRESIS DIAGNOSIS OR SUBSEQUENT THERAPY WOULD COME MY WAY. INSTEAD, WE MANAGED. WE SCRUBBED & HID & KEPT THIS AS A SHAMEFUL SECRET, BIDING OUR TIME BETWEEN PAINFUL EPISODES & DOCTOR'S VISITS.

There were a lot of enemies when I was a kid
My stepfather, Ed,
My teachers at school,
" Knock
Knock "
... And the truancy officer.

Mom!
SLAM!
grumble grumble
who was that?
grumble grumble

I didn't go to school much
z z z z
time to get up.
C'mon.
I'm sick.
It hurts so bad!
IN THE FOURTH GRADE I WAS ABSENT OVER 40 DAYS IN ONE YEAR.
IT DIDN'T TAKE MUCH. A SORE THROAT OR SOME TEARS.
Fine.
I'll call you at noon to check in.
click
sniff
yes!

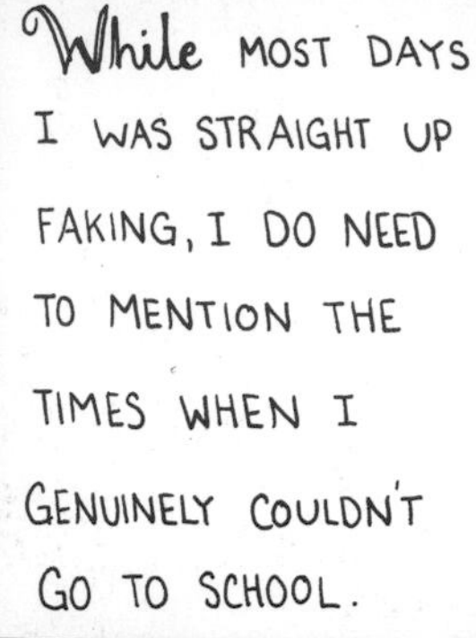
While MOST DAYS I WAS STRAIGHT UP FAKING, I DO NEED TO MENTION THE TIMES WHEN I GENUINELY COULDN'T GO TO SCHOOL.

THE STOMACH PAINS CAUGHT UP TO ME.

Come on, Nick.
I can't get up.
My stomach hurts.

DAYS AND WEEKS OF NOT GOING TO THE BATHROOM LED TO MORNINGS OF SEVERE IMMOBILITY.
No no no no no

I told him my dad died of colon cancer.
SOMETIMES I'D WAIT IT OUT IN BED ALL DAY. SOMETIMES WE DROVE TO THE HOSPITAL.

THIS WAS NOT ONE OF THOSE DAYS.
I GOT WELL-TRAINED IN LYING DURING MY DAYS OFF FROM SCHOOL. THEY INVOLVED FAKE NOTES, FORGED CHECKS & CODED PHONE CALLS.
Click
Click
?
click
?

rrring!
rrrring!
ED WAS HOME FOR AN HOUR + A HALF
Hello?
MOM AND I HAD A CODE FOR DAYTIME PHONE CALLS. RING TWICE, HANG UP, CALL BACK.
Hi, Sabine.
Just taking lunch.
Why you calling here in the middle of the day? ...Nick's at school.
hmm.
mmm hmm.
Okay. Bye.
WE DEVELOPED THE CODE IN CASE ED CALLED HOME MIDDAY. OR CREDITORS. OR SCHOOL. JUST SO I KNEW WHEN IT WAS OKAY TO ANSWER THE PHONE.

?
hmm.
whine
whine
Quit it.
Arp!
SLAM!
Clop-Clomp-
Clomp...
SLAM!
Phew!
I can't believe he came home!
Where were you?
In my closet!
Good Job.
That was a close one.
IT WAS OUR SECRET.

Err Ah ERRR!*

*Cock-A-Doodle Doo

BAWK BAWK BAWK BAWK
bwaaah bwaa
BWAAAAAAA
Shut. UP!
Bwaa?
BWAAAAA
Okay Okay
BWAAAAH!
grumble grumble
CHICKEN FÜD
Here. Now be Quiet!
!
Bwaaa.

What happened to you?
Beija, come.
bwah?
SLAM!
Here.
bwaa?
?
If you take this away I have no one to escort my fears to the place I have built as my fear fort

no reason to wait through the winter's sad discourse
Bwaaa
Bwaaaa.
I'll be in soon. Chill out!

http://www.hotmail.com/abcdefghijklmn

INBOX FROM: RADARVONKRONE@GMAIL.COM
TRASH TO: NG@KITEMAIL.COM
Drafts
Folders

Dear Nicole,
The only thing I don't miss about Portland is the rain. I want to move back. I need to finish some things here first.

Our band is practicing all the time now for our tour. Here is what I wish I was doing instead- eating this nice pumpkin pie.

Would you consider visiting me? I know it's a lot to ask. I could get a ticket whenever you want. Attaching a photo.

SWAK,
Radar

Radar-
This morning I walked outside & found my chicken Mabel's head pecked open by the dastardly Laverne.
She is currently awaiting treatment in the bathroom wing of the Georges Infirmary.

In other news, I need to bake a cake for a friend today.
Are there ever songs you hear that just tear at your heart? Like, cut your Achilles tendon & make you fall to the floor? Just wondering.
Sometimes I hear this one band & I feel that way. Sometimes I hear them & it's okay.
Another time, we can discuss.
I would like to eat cake with you. Or pumpkin pie. See you soon.
xoxo, N.G.

Send.
Cluck Cluck
I will heal you.

The only person to ever mention my father by name was an old lady at my grandfather's 90th birthday party

I'm a friend of your grandfather's.
I remember when you where this big!
Your mother is Sabine?
yes.
... and your father's name is David.
mmm hmm.
? David.
?
David.
?
gulp
David.
?
I remember when you stayed here as a baby.
Oh, everybody loved you!
"Little Pee-Pee"!
hmm

Yes, I remember your father...
You do?
heyyy, Estelle
oh, Excuse me, Nickie.
Oh, Hello, Agnes!
David.
??
"Dad"
DAVID?
His ACTUAL NAME WAS NEVER SPOKEN AGAIN.
EVER.

My bio dad was only ever mentioned a few times.
Sigh . Your Dad & I used to sing this song to each other.
even though we ain't got money, I'm so in love with ya honey
We didn't have much, but we were in love.
Look at the picture I found!
Oh yeah.
He had a really rough childhood...
Your dad ran away when he was 13 & survived on his own as a little hoodlum!
See this hat? I wore one just like it to your dad's funeral.
It was so sad.
Poor Dad.
I NEVER QUESTIONED WHY SHE WAS THE ONLY NARRATOR, OR SUSPECTED THAT HER INFORMATION WOULD ONE DAY PROVE UNRELIABLE.

I was bitten by Lambchop within an hour of my arrival in L.A.
Make yourself comfortable. I have to let the dogs out.
grrrrrrrrr,

I'll do it!
Go on, dogs!
RADAR FLEW ME OUT TO VISIT. I WAS IMMEDIATELY CHARMED BY HER HOUSE AND HERD.

You too, Grandpa.

arrr!

shit!

Are you okay?
yeah!
I COVERED UP MY WOUND SO THAT RADAR WOULD THINK ANIMALS LIKED ME.
I'm still trying to get their names straight!
Look at this!
wow!
here.

Her front tooth was made of metal.

And her room smelled like red ginger.

I liked to watch her walk. This petite person with a masculine sort of amble.

The thing that got me, though, was the sweet lilt in her voice as she called the name Lou.

And the warm excited smile as he neared her, ears flapping, racing to meet his queen.

The kindness in her for her animals, their complete devotion to her...

I fell in love with Radar for that reason alone.

Honestly,
THAT WAS IT.
I THOUGHT I COULD SHARE IN THE DOGS' GRACE.
What is it? Are you OKay?
Yeah.
I'm just thirsty...
you don't have to...

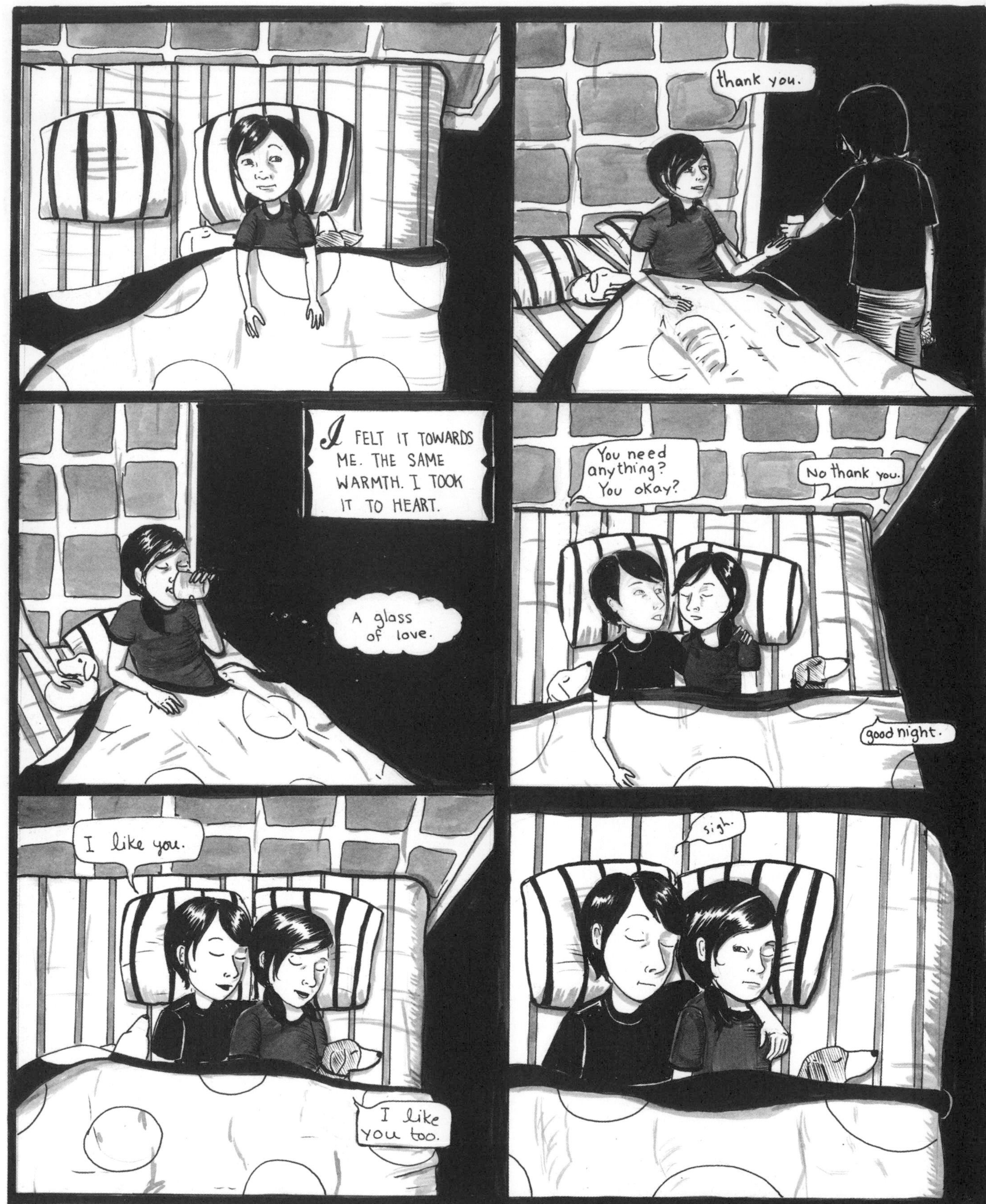
thank you.
I FELT IT TOWARDS ME. THE SAME WARMTH. I TOOK IT TO HEART.
A glass of love.
You need anything? You okay?
No thank you.
good night.
I like you.
I like you too.
sigh.

Divorce
I WAS GLAD WHEN MY MOTHER FINALLY BROKE IT OFF WITH ED.
Nickie, we're getting a divorce.
okay.
WHAT WITH ALL THE FIGHTING,
B*TCH!
THE CHOKING,
...Nickie...
CALL 911
AND OBVIOUS TERROR,
OPEN THIS DOOR!!!
...Four Five Four Laurel Park Lane...
IT SEEMED ONLY NATURAL THAT SHE SHOULD LEAVE HIM.
Knock Knock
You can come out now.

He's gone.
AND WE COULD GO SOMEWHERE TO BE ALONE.
mom?
Thank you, sweetie.
Did he go to jail?
no.
He went to get a drink.
oh.
JUST THE TWO OF US.

Naturally,
I was shocked when she took me to therapy.
Let's talk about the divorce.
!
SMACK!
What was that?
A...
A bird just flew into the window!

Oh, really?
hmm.
So anyway,
the divorce.
No, like it hit the glass really hard!
We should see if it's okay!
Did it?
Well, okay.
hmm.
I don't see him.

...So, I'll bet he's fine.
ahem
Like Most Things, MY MOTHER DIDN'T MAKE ME GO TO THE THERAPIST MORE THAN ONCE.
How'd it go?
I hate 'ER.
A bird hit the glass of the window and she didn't even DO anything.
hmm.
I don't see why I have to go anyway.
I wanted you to get a divorce!
...Ed sucks.
hmm.

bark bark
Hi!
Our new house will be way cooler than this one, Chatters.
Chatters is staying here with Daddy.
but Why?!??
Because she's his dog and I said so.
I Hate That Dog.
actual thought

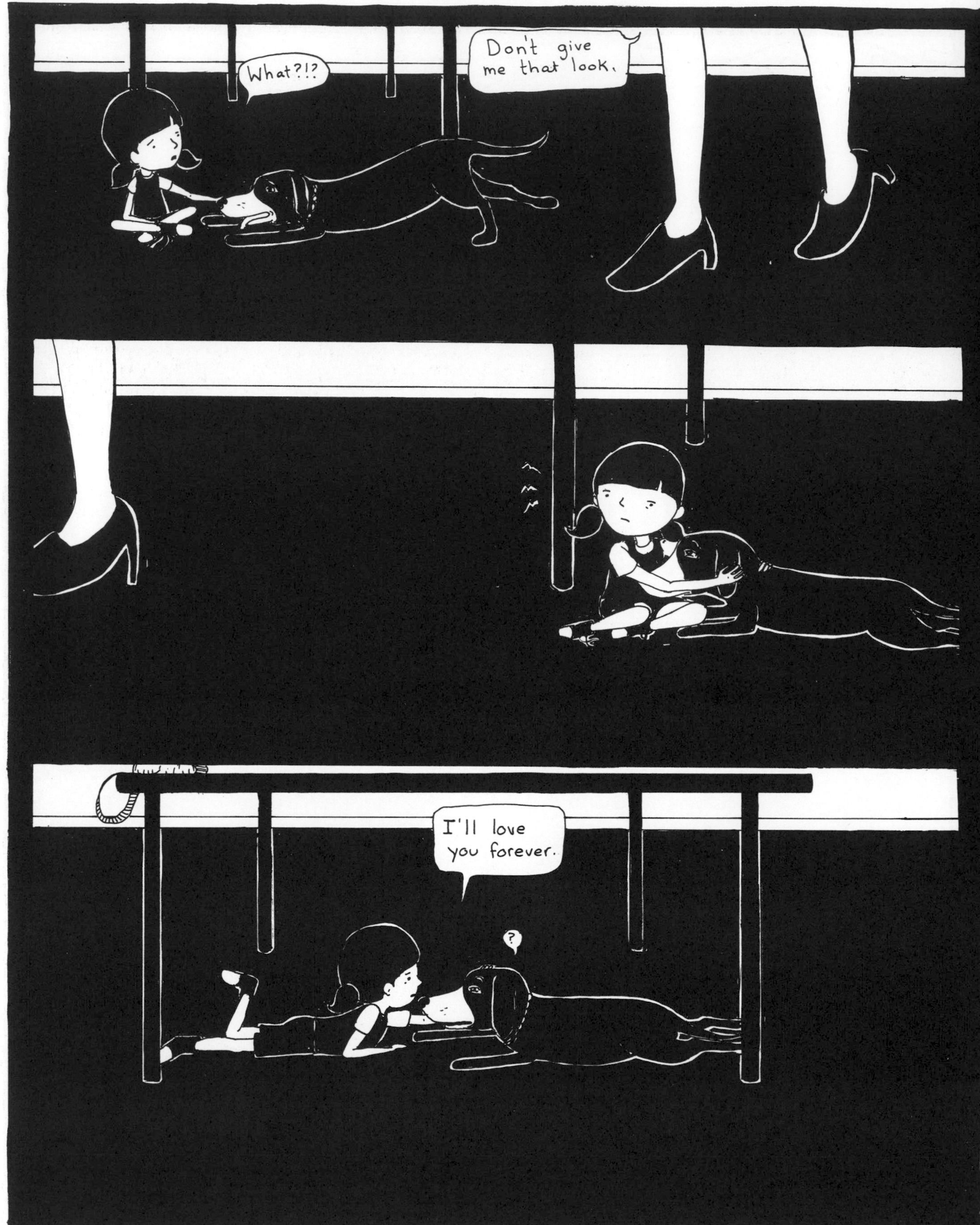
What?!?
Don't give me that look.
I'll love you forever.
?

Gizmo
What should we name him?
WE HADN'T LEFT ED'S HOUSE AS EXPECTED.
I don't know_
I guess he looks like that guy from Gremlins...
...Gizmo?
I MEAN, WE LEFT-
BUT WE MOVED IN WITH MOM'S BOYFRIEND, PETE.
Ack! Okay, Gizmo.
Don't you have something to say to Pete?
thanks, Pete.
Well, you're welcome.

I ONLY SAW ED ONCE OR TWICE POST-DIVORCE.
AS VISITATIONS WANED, SO DID MY MEMORIES OF CHATTERS.
SHE WAS REPLACED, AND I SOON BECAME CONSUMED WITH GIZMO.
SQUAT TEAM
HE WAS NOT ONLY MY BUSINESS PARTNER, BUT ALSO MY FRIEND.
I WALKED HIM AROUND OUR NEW NEIGHBORHOOD, ADVERTISING OUR DOG WALKING SERVICE.
WE RODE DOWN TRAILS
What if my real dad was a king?
AND SCHEMED TO CREATE A HISTORY AND A CAREER TOGETHER.

I could be Princess Nicolette. No... Nicolettia.
...Princess Nicolettia.
?
It always seemed lackluster to dream about my father.
More exciting to think of Gizmo as Benji. More realistic at least.
Come, Benji.
Pop!

WELCOME
Brrring!

Hello?
Oh, Hi, Mom.
drink
drink
Yeah, I can make myself dinner.
Where you going?
You're going to the Melting Pot!?!
!!!
but we were supposed to go there.
Remember when I saw the ad & told you about it...?
...and you're going with Pete?!?!?
This is SO....
Okay, Okay Whatever.
BYE.
SLAM!!!

AAAAAUGH!
SLAM SLAM SLAM
NO, GIZMO.
BAD.
err?
GO LAY DOWN.
?
Here.

Stupid, Stupid, Stupid.
I hate her.
She barely even KNOWS him and she's taking him to our place, MY place...

♥?

I CAME TO PORTLAND ON A LARK, IMPERVIOUS TO THE COLD SPLATTER OF ITS LONG WET WINTERS. ALL I SAW WERE MOUNTAINS AND BICYCLES AND SOMETHING MORE MY OWN THAN KANSAS.

I PUT MY DOG IN THE FRONT SEAT AND TIED MY FURNITURE INTO THE BED OF THE PICKUP TRUCK, BEVERLY HILLBILLIES STYLE.

I CATALOGUED EVERY DETAIL OF MY NEW CITY IN A COMIC. THE WEATHER, THE FRIENDS, AND THE GINGERBREAD MANOR:- A DRAFTY VICTORIAN MADE OF DARK WOOD AND FLOWERED WALLPAPER.

I Celebrated
THE RELEASE OF MY BOOK WITH THE DOOR TO MY BEDROOM CLOSED.
I SHARED VIETNAMESE TAKE-OUT WITH BEIJA AND MABEL.
bwaaah?
A rainy
NIGHT OF DRIZZLE AND THE LIGHT RAIL'S CHIME AS IT DROVE BY OUR HOUSE, ONE BLOCK EAST.
BEIJA WAS AFRAID OF MABEL, &
Bwaaaah
I WAS THEIR ONLY FRIEND IN COMMON.

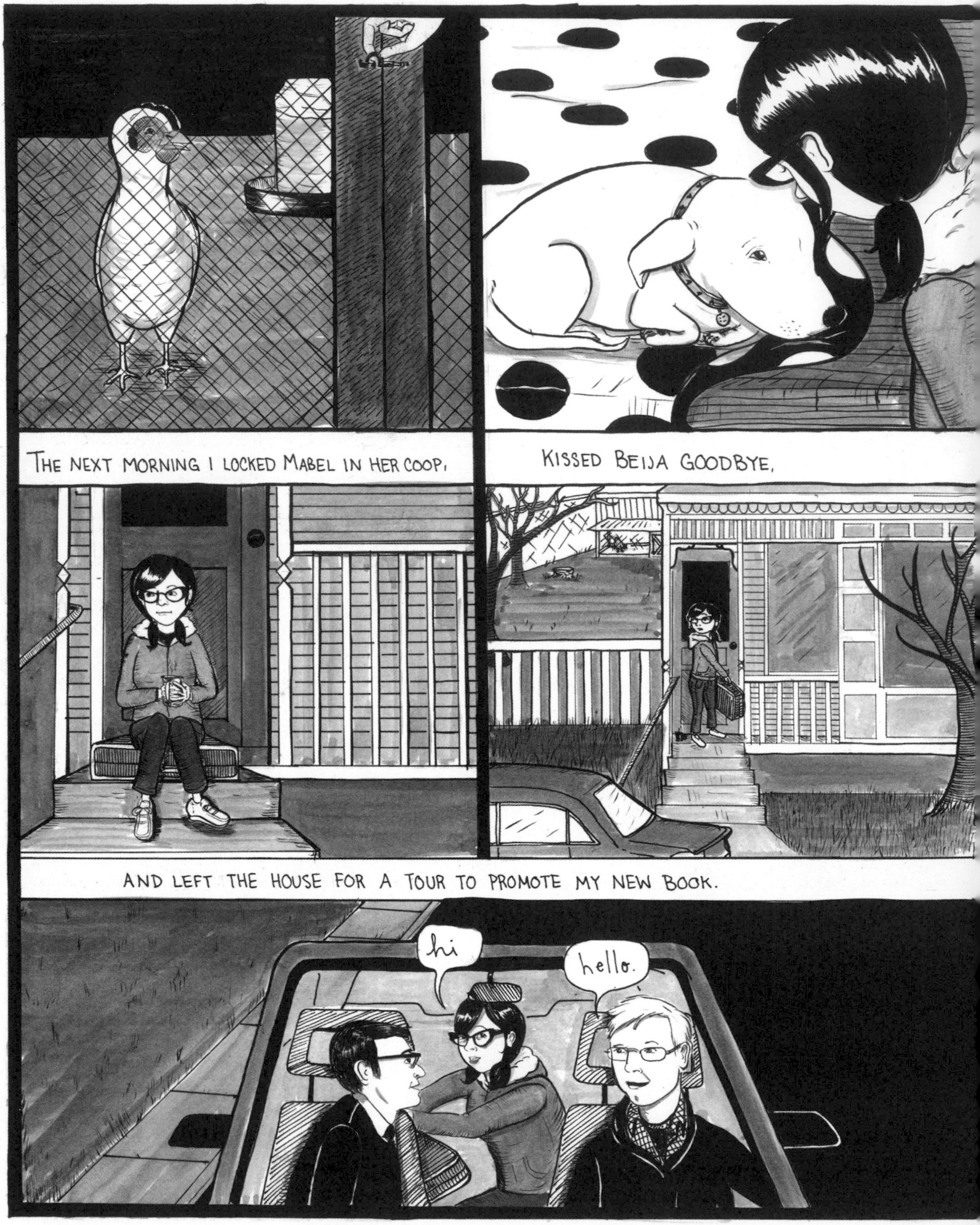

THE NEXT MORNING I LOCKED MABEL IN HER COOP,

KISSED BEIJA GOODBYE,

AND LEFT THE HOUSE FOR A TOUR TO PROMOTE MY NEW BOOK.

RINNNG
RINNNG
Z Z Z
hello?
I GOT A FLIP PHONE FOR OUR JOURNEY.
BOOKS

Guess who was at our show last night?
Who?
Robin Williams!
Our tours were very different.
Well guess who was at our show?
Who?
Jessica Tandy!
Who?
The old lady from Driving Miss Daisy?
Star Studded!
Really?
... Just kidding.
Radar with two bands & me with 2 authors.
I told my sister to go see your show in San Francisco.
..did you see her?
I did...
She came to see you? I'm so glad!
...yeah.
So.... how was it?
invincible summer
Books

Your sister's really intense, Nicole.
Oh...Okay.
..And she really loves you.
And she has something she really needs to tell you.
....
What do you mean?
What is it?
I don't know, she wouldn't tell me.
Did they sleep together?
...Why is she being so cryptic?
invincible summer
?
Anyway, I want to see you.
rest area

I want to see you too.
Will you think about visiting me again?
secret?
sure.
MEN

A Shiba Inu ATE MY GLASSES IN CONNECTICUT.
Ooops!
Toby, No!
Sorry About that.
He was eating your underwear!

?
hmmm
secret
what is my
lie
she loves you
your sister has something to tell you
david?
Are these your glasses?
I'm so sorry.
hmm!?!
I found them in the yard.

crack
Fuck off.
You guys can stay at my mom's house.
She has these really expensive dogs there.
Oh, I love dogs!
He's such a bad boy. Come here, Toby!
A $2000 DOG ATE MY GLASSES.
Here. I'll give you my email. You let me know how much it costs to fix them.
um....
Well, they're antiques, but... hmm...
Maybe they'll be okay.
(THE OWNER NEVER PAID ME BACK.)

I WANT TO TELL YOU WHAT HAPPENED ON TOUR AFTER THE DOG ATE MY GLASSES.
OPEN
events
hello?
Hi!
Oh... what is it? ...
Just feathers in the garden? .....
Mabel died.
IT FELT LIKE IT WAS ALL MY FAULT FOR LEAVING HOME.
I'm sorry I'm sorry
I'm sorry I'm sor
I'm sorry I'm sorr
I'm sorry I'm sorry
I'm sorry I'm sorry
I'm sorry I'm sorry. I'm sorry
Dear Mabel, I couldn't keep you safe I wasn't there I'm so sorry.
?What if Liz is my mom & my mom is my Grandmother??
ONCE MY CHICKEN WAS DEAD & MY GLASSES HAD BEEN CHEWED, I STUCK TO MY DEN IN THE BACKSEAT. THIS GAVE ME TIME TO MEDITATE ON THE SECRET. MY GUESSES ALL LEANED ON THE TABLOID SIDE OF THINGS. IT HELPED TO KEEP MY MIND OFF OF MABEL.

HALLOWEEN ROCK-A-THON
HALLOWEEN ROCK-A-THON
HALLOWEEN
TONIGHT
TICKETS
WILL CALL
HALLOWEEN
MEGA SHOW
I DIDN'T WANT TO GO HOME AFTER TOUR.
I BOUGHT A TICKET TO L.A. INSTEAD.
TICKETS
SOLD OUT
gulp
yes?
h-hi. I'M looking for Ra-
Let her in! That's Radar's friend.

!!!
wait.
I have something for you.
here.
Is it a doughnut?
You pointed those out once... I remembered.
?
I thought you might need a new pair....
......You like 'em?
...I can take them back if you.....

Oh.
Thank you.

Mom met Pete at the gym,
An Italian stallion!
and referred to him as
Cool!
HE WORE GOLD CHAINS & DROVE A SPORTS CAR.
I got you something.
thanks
Okay, Nick, hop in.
maybe you can thank Pete by naming your toy after him.
I LIKED THE SPORTS CAR AS MUCH AS ANYONE, BUT UNFORTUNATELY THERE WAS NO BACKSEAT.

WHEN WE TOOK OUR FIRST ROAD TRIP, I WAS FOLDED IN THE BACK WINDOW.

I BROUGHT EDMONDO + GIZMO, & DID PUPPET SHOWS FOR THE OTHER CARS ON THE FLORIDA HIGHWAY.

PETE TRADED IN HIS SPORTS CAR FOR SOMETHING BIGGER WHEN WE MOVED TO KANSAS.

MOM & PETE WOULD LEAVE THE DUPLEX EVERY TUESDAY NIGHT FOR CATHOLIC CONVERSION CLASSES.

I SAT AT HOME & SNACKED, ROLLERBLADED, & MADE CONVERSATION WITH GIZMO.

I DID SLOW MOTION DANCE INTERPRETATIONS TO THEIR NATALIE COLE CDS WHEN THEY GOT HOME & MADE DINNER.

SINCE THEY COULDN'T GET MARRIED IN THE CATHOLIC CHURCH, MOM & PETE BOOKED A TRIP TO JAMAICA.

THEY WERE WED ON THE BEACH, IN A PRIVATE CEREMONY WITNESSED ONLY BY SEAGULLS AND HOTEL STAFF.

I WAS BACK IN KANSAS, BEING STORED AT A FRIEND'S HOUSE.

ONCE THEY WERE OFFICIALLY CATHOLIC & MARRIED, SO WAS I (CATHOLIC, NOT MARRIED).

I ATTENDED CATHOLIC YOUTH CLASSES IN THE CHURCH BASEMENT,

AND WAS CONFIRMED IN A NEW FLOWERY DRESS MOM PURCHASED FOR THE OCCASION. A NEW COSTUME FOR A NEW SCENE.

WE STARTED HANGING OUT WITH HOME-OWNERS & TALKED ABOUT ENLISTING IN CATHOLIC SCHOOL.

I TRIED TO LEARN CHEERLEADING JUMPS SO THAT I MIGHT QUALIFY FOR THE SQUAD AT MY NEW SCHOOL.
(note: I failed at this, remained earthbound.)

THIS WAS OUR NEW LIFE.

NOTHING BEFORE KANSAS EXISTED.

PETE EVEN TRIED TO ADOPT ME. NEW LIFE, NEW NAME.

I SAID NO. (I STILL FEEL LIKE A JERK FOR THIS, BUT IT MADE SENSE AT THE TIME.)

A NEW DAD DIDN'T SOUND LIKE STABILITY TO ME. IT SOUNDED LIKE BECOMING THE PROPERTY OF ANOTHER ADULT WHOSE WHIMS AND CHANGES WOULD AFFECT MY LIFE.
I WANTED TO BELONG TO MYSELF.

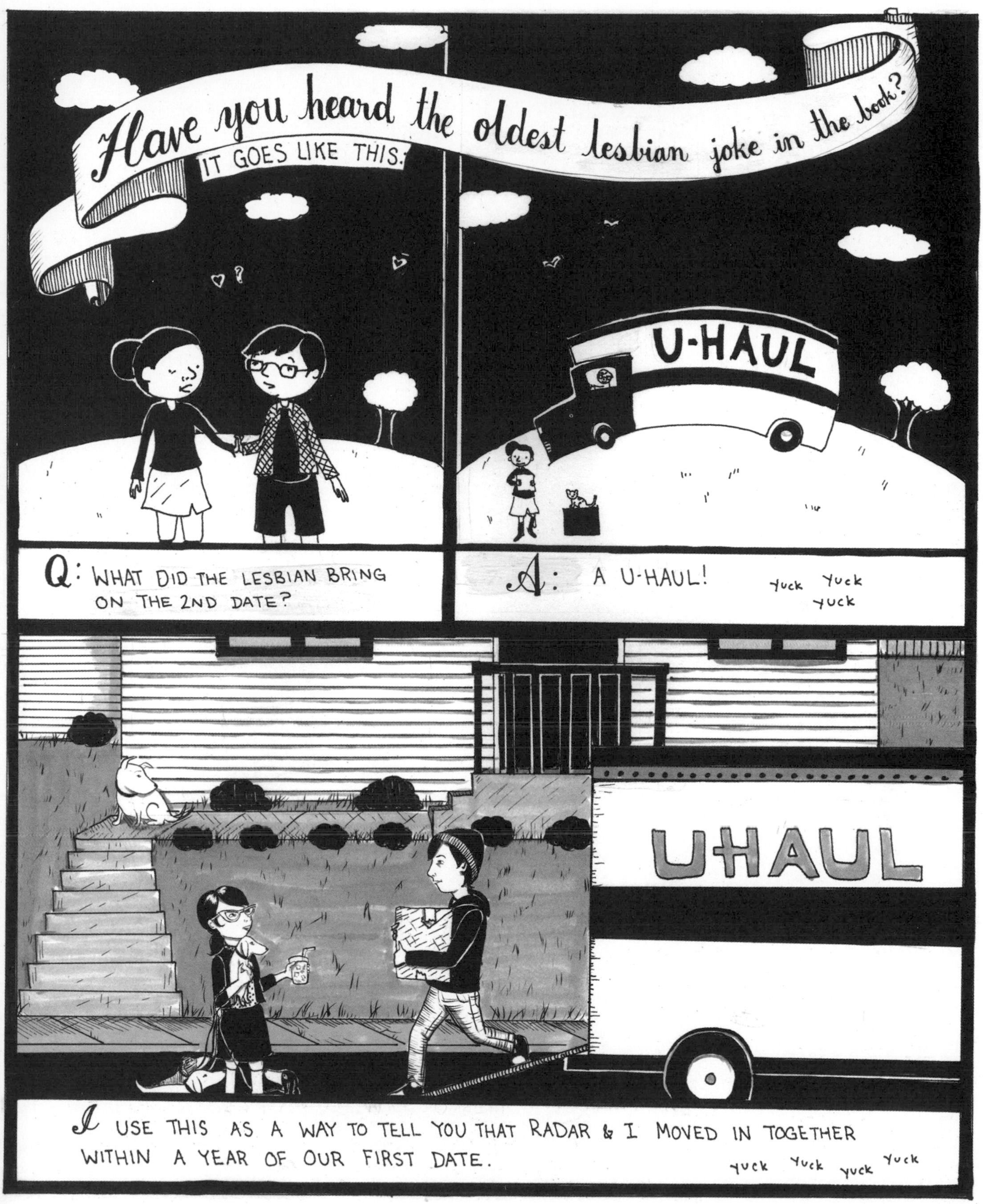

Have you heard the oldest lesbian joke in the book?

IT GOES LIKE THIS:

Q: WHAT DID THE LESBIAN BRING ON THE 2ND DATE?

A: A U-HAUL!

yuck yuck yuck

I USE THIS AS A WAY TO TELL YOU THAT RADAR & I MOVED IN TOGETHER WITHIN A YEAR OF OUR FIRST DATE.

yuck yuck yuck yuck

Four new dogs in one new house
Lou, No!
DOGS ON THE COUCH,
CHASING THE CHICKENS,
He was there first.
Move it!
Grrrr
LAYING IN MY SPOT,
sniff
PEEING ON THE FLOOR,
grrr
Arf!
Awooo!
Arf!
Arf
Arf!
Arf!
AND RUNNING AT THE DOOR.
THIS WAS LIFE WITH MY NEW SMALL ROOMMATES.

QUICKLY, I MUST TELL YOU-
We started a Band
Darkened grows
seasons slowing ... forest
what's that spell?
I SANG, MADE MERCH, & BOOKED SHOWS.
RADAR PLAYED GUITAR & WROTE SONGS.
you're frozen in between the fantasy ...and what is real. Dear owl how can
How was that?
Sigh
SHE RECORDED OUR DEMO IN THE BASEMENT. WE PRACTICED EVERY DAY.
You didn't like it?
It was flat.
what is "flat"?
I'll do it again.

How was that?
rrrr...
bzzzt
PRACTICING EVERY DAY DIDN'T LEAVE MUCH TIME FOR MY OTHER FRIENDS.
VERONA MAUSS
GEORGES I MISS YOU. WHERE R U? WANT 2 GET DINNER?
WED. 6:16 PM
Options Reply Back
Let's just move on to the next song, okay?
Hey-

Radar was a little jealous of Verona, so I never pushed it.

I came straight home from work every night, took care of the dogs, & practiced my parts.

I had Verona over for pancakes when we moved into the new house. It resulted in a bit of a fight.

How was your time with your friend?
Really nice!
Didn't you make pancakes?
Yeah!
Where are they?
Oh, we ate them all.
Well, what am I supposed to eat?
I don't know...
have you checked the fridge?
That's not the point.
What?
The point is that you made food for her - and none for me.
I didn't know I was supposed to make food for you - it was a breakfast date.
Oh, A Date?!?

No, not a date-date... you know what I mean.
No, Nicole, I don't think I do know what you mean.
You invite some girl over who you used to sleep with, you feed her Our Food, and leave me out!
I haven't seen her in months! I wanted to have private friend times!
Yeah, I'll bet.
What are you talking about, we barely even dated, and-
I DIDN'T SEE MUCH OF VERONA AFTER THAT.
SLAM!
I DECIDED TO SPEND MORE TIME ON THE BAND INSTEAD.

?Fact or Fiction?
After six months of playing shows, we decided to go on a short tour of the West Coast.
SLAM
FF CDs
COMMUNITY ART SPACE
ZINES
SILKSCREENING
Letterpress
F?F
F?F
CDs

I PRINTED THE COVERS TO OUR DEMO CD MYSELF AND SCAVENGED IN THRIFT STORES UNTIL I FOUND FIFTY SHIRTS AND DRESSES TO EMBLAZE WITH OUR LOGO.

WE HAD AN AGENDA WITH THIS TOUR BEYOND SELLING MERCHANDISE AND PLAYING SHOWS.

WE WERE GOING TO END UP IN SAN FRANCISCO, WHERE MY SISTER LIZ LIVED. IT WAS TIME FOR ME TO ASK HER ABOUT WHAT SHE'D BEEN WANTING TO TELL ME.

Are you nervous?
For our shows? Never!
I mean about your sister.
SHE'D MENTIONED IT AGAIN TO RADAR IN THE PRECEDING MONTHS- SOMETHING BIG LIZ HAD BEEN KEEPING FROM ME.
Oh. Well, it just kind of blows my mind.
She could be my Mom and my Mom could be my Grandma-
and that would go along with what the psychic said...
...Or my Dad could be alive and, well, the psychic would also be correct.
WAIT- Why would you think she's your Mom???
It makes sense! I've always felt a stronger bond with her than anyone in the family,
and we have the same mouth.
And my Mom had lots of creepy guys around then...
Maybe one of them raped her & she had me when she was twelve.
Nicole!
Well! It would make sense to keep that a secret.

I don't think she's your Mom.
Okay, so maybe my Dad's just alive, and-
And?
I don't know what.
But How weird would it be if the psychic were right?
Pretty weird.
This is the time, Nicole. You can't hide from this forever.
FORD
Welcome to California

Our tour drives were fun.
Okay, left here.
WE MADE A GOOD BUSINESS TEAM.
I think I've played here before -
FORD
EXIT
Where is everybody?
But OUR SHOWS WERE SCARCELY ATTENDED. THE TOUR FELT A LITTLE CURSED.
What about the posters?
I was, like, so busy this week with work, man... I told a few friends, but...
Radar! I just saw Bob Hoskins walking down the street!
Who?
you know-
I KEPT SEEING THE POSTERS I'D SENT TO PROMOTERS SITTING IN THEIR CARS, NOT STAPLED TO A POLE, JUST ABANDONED.
OUR ONE BIG SHOW WAS IN LOS ANGELES, THE SITE OF OUR INITIAL ROMANCE.

IT WAS THE ONLY PACKED HOUSE OF THE TRIP; BUT AS WE SET UP BEHIND THE CURTAIN, SOMETHING WAS WRONG.
Something's wrong.
What do you mean?
The computer won't work.
2 DAYS BEFORE
woops!
computer brain
gulp
Uh... are you sure the volume's up?
Hey, are you guys almost ready? The venue's closing soon.
Just a suggestion!
gulp
Hey Radar-
MUTE
You're kidding.
click
MUTE

We played for ten glorious minutes.
43

Liz's Coming Out Story
Liz!
breathe
breathe
Ticketed passengers only.
BUR
Good to have you home, honey.
Look at you! So slim!
Mom....
I made you grape leaves like you like, and Kibbeh and we've got olives and good bread and I thought we could visit tonight and -
Sooo, how's San Francisco?
It's... good.
Any hot guys?

Nooo....
Well, you're so beautiful you don't need to worry about that.
Mom...
yessss??
I'm in love with a woman.
heh?
You're kidding.
Her name is Frederika and she's
So what are you now, a Lesbian?
Honey, you're too beautiful to be a Lesbian!
What about Brad??
I'm bisexual.
Ha!

Why? Why would you do this? A dyke, Liz? Are you a DYKE?
I can't even imagine how you could even make Love with a woman.
Mom...
EW!- Dirty FINGERS, STINKY PUSSIES!
Mom! Listen-
No, Liz, you Listen to Me.
No daughter of mine is going to be a DYKE.
Sob
4FS 679
And that is how it went down
"The verbal beating of my life," AS LIZ RECALLS IT.
I DIDN'T IMAGINE MY COMING OUT WOULD GO ANY BETTER,
LIZ AND MOM STOPPED SPEAKING SHORTLY THEREAFTER.
AND SO...
4FS 679
I DIDN'T TELL MY MOM.

San Francisco
El Rio
your dive
thirty one fifty eight
?FACT OR FICTION?

Why does nothing ever turn out like it should

i hope there's still time to set things right

clap
clap
clap
clap
clap
Nicole J. Georges!
you were great!
Oh, thanks, Liz!

MY SISTER LIZ BOUGHT ALL OF OUR MERCH- SHIRTS, A BOOK, CDs, AND A HOMEMADE DRESS WITH OUR LOGO ON IT.

IT WAS THE LAST NIGHT OF OUR VERY TUMULTUOUS TOUR.

HERE'S WHAT I REMEMBER FROM THIS NIGHT....
I CAME RIGHT OUT AND ASKED IT.
Tonight was really good, I thought.
Yeah, it was better than I expected.
WE WALKED UP THE HILL TO MY SISTER'S HOUSE,
AND GOT TO TALKING OVER CORONAS AS THE COOL NIGHT BLEW IN THROUGH OPEN KITCHEN WINDOWS.

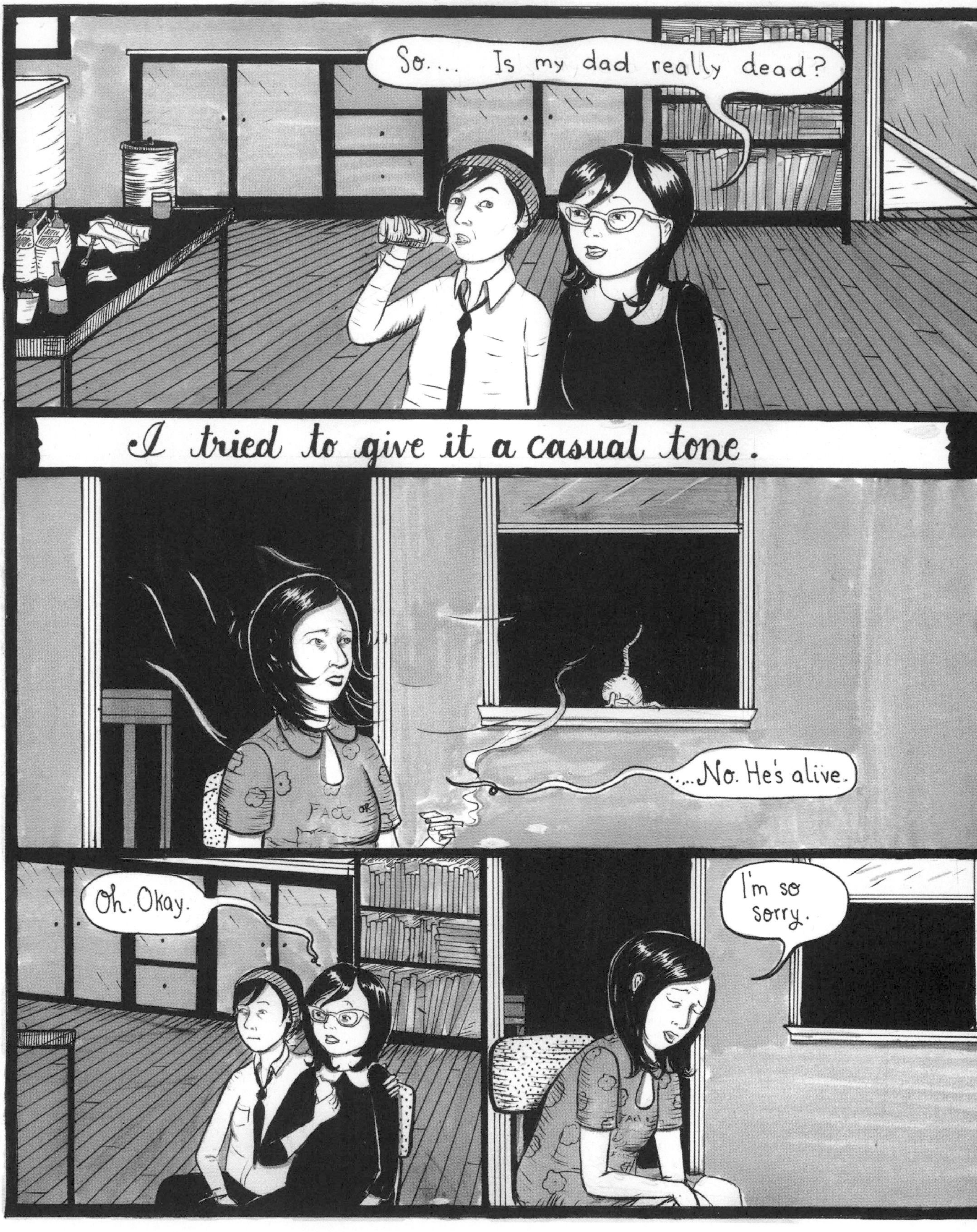

I tried to give it a casual tone.

....No. He's alive.

Oh. Okay.

I'm so sorry.

Please don't hate me for keeping this from you.
THAT WAS IT.
LIZ'S BIG SECRET.
THAT WAS ALL.
I wanted to tell you, but...
Do you hate me?
No!
IT HAD NEVER EVEN OCCURRED TO ME TO HATE MY SISTER.

It's way better than what I thought!
ha... ha
I thought maybe you were my mom & Mom was my grandma!
THERE WAS A LOT TO TALK ABOUT.

My dad, from what I was told, was a con man.
What are you girls doing?
Work for David.
A bookie
?
Let me see that.
?!
Bookie sheets!
I need to leave for a while.
Now?
They found out where I am. I need to go.
A CROOKED BUSINESSMAN,

And A PISTOL-PACKING JEWEL THIEF.
What's that?
It's protection.
for my friend.
Here, I brought you something.

Where did you get these?
THIS IS WHAT I KNOW.
I THINK IT WAS EXCITING.
I THINK IT GOT OLD.
David, I can't accept these.
No?
FINE.
I got them for YOU.
SLAM!

ONE WEEK LATER

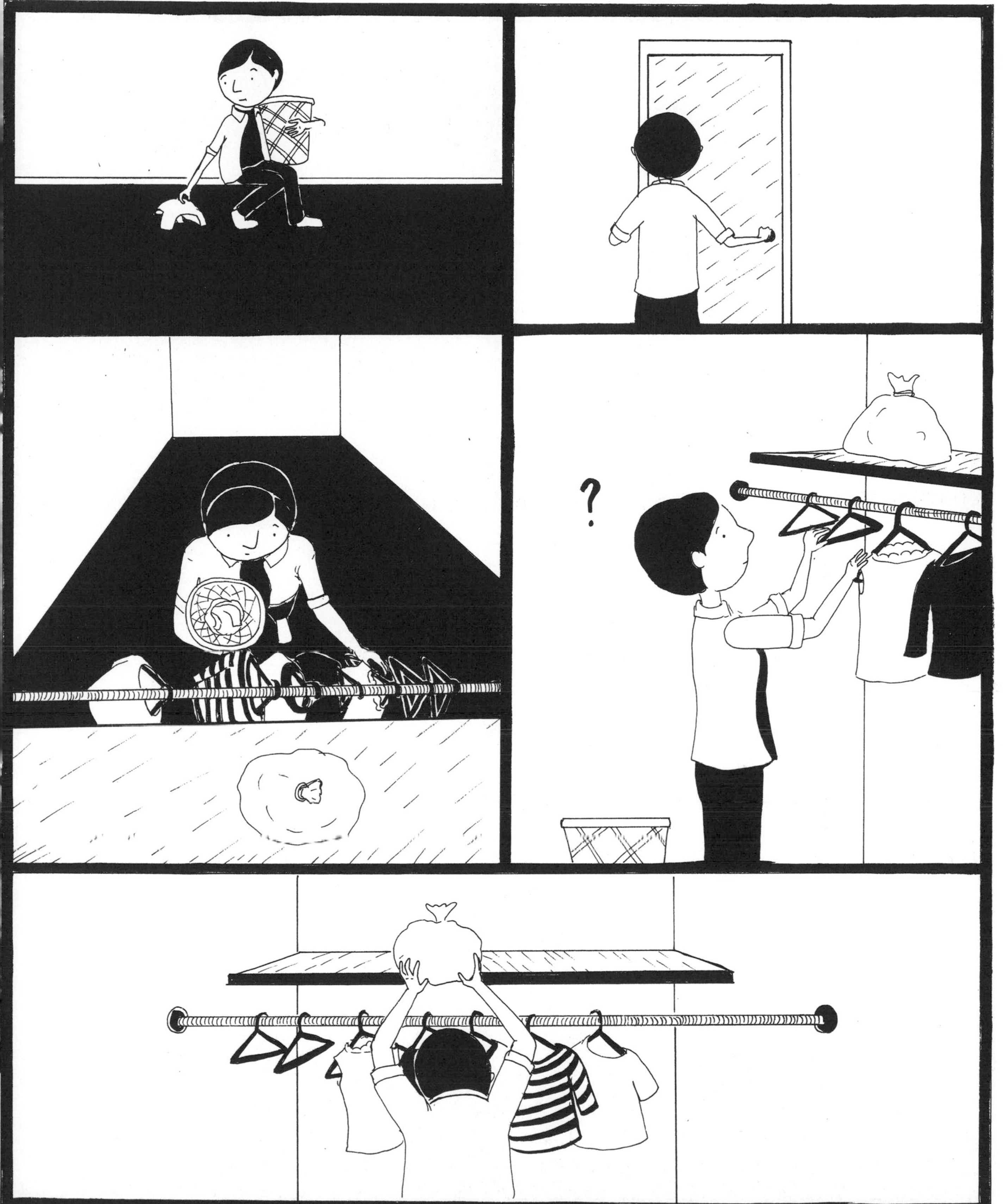

GASP!
Sob

David was the love of Mom's life (for a while)
DANGEROUS!
mysterious
charismatic!
PASSIONATE!
BUT HE ENDED UP ON THE COUCH
HE'D BEEN INJURED AT WORK, AND FELL INTO A DEEP, DARK DEPRESSION.
Ahem
tap tap tap
ALMOST OVERNIGHT, THE QUICK-STEPPING BREADWINNER BECAME AN ALBATROSS TO MY MOTHER.
THIS IS PROBABLY WHY SHE LEFT HIM.

...and Mom moved on
Oh, Sabine,
I love you.
I'll return in an hour.
yes.
Mom, who is that?
It's Faisal.
He's a prince!
?
Honey, he's going to make us very rich.
You guys will be princesses!
What's that look for?

Well...
Where's David?
He's gone. He's not coming back.
giggle
What about Nickie?
What about her?
What if she wants to know about her dad?
He's out of the picture.
...tell her he died.
?
?
What do we say he died from?
Sigh.
I don't know.... Colon Cancer.
?
?

Ding Dong
Now Wipe those Looks off your faces.
but, Mom, Faisal is a very good man!
Don't you disrespect me!
You think it's easy raising three kids alone?
I work my butt off for you guys, and I'm allowed to have a little fun if I want to.
And anyway, Faisal is Royalty!

You selfish brats wouldn't understand.
Sabine?
Coming!
SLAM!
Hello, beautiful.
GIRLS! Come say Hello!

Juniors
Juniors
Juniors
Why won't any-one talk about it?
-Uncle Wally, Aunt Janet, They all played dumb. They said you must be mistaken.
Old Syrian families keep each other's secrets, Nicole.
They're like the mafia.
yeah, I was like, why would you guys lie to me about that?
We wouldn't!
That's just some family bullshit.
..that's what I'm saying. The Georges are not your family.
We have to build our own families.

They've all been lying to you.
that's right.
It's really fucked up, Nicole.
I talked to Mom the other day, but I didn't bring it up.
I didn't know what to say.
It just feels really intense, like, I know how she'll react.
She'll just defend herself.
...you know?

yawwn...
It's just too much.
I don't know how you and Meg can still talk to her.
Mom lied to you, Nicole.
That is such a messed up thing to do to a kid.
I've told Nicole I think she should stop talking to her.
Totally. That woman is a Nightmare.
YAWWWN—

Well, she's a lot different now than when you were growing up.
mm hmm.
Why would you want someone like this in your life?
well...
I'll think about it.
You obviously can't handle talking about this.
Look, you're totally shutting down.
No I'm not. I'm just hungry.

IT'S TRUE. I WAS LYING TO LIZ. I DIDN'T KNOW IT AT THE TIME.

Have you heard of fainting goats?

Fainting Goats

A fainting goat is a breed of goat born with a genetic condition called Myotonia Congenita. This causes the goat's muscles to lock up when startled. It will then fall over and lay very stiff for five to ten seconds.

Though th never fully lose conso sness, this gives the appe ce of a "faint", name.

According to writer Robert Lamb: "Younger goats are more prone to fall over and tumble when startled, but as they grow older, many eventually manage to avoid falling over altogether during an episode. They simply run away on stiffened legs."

"Older goats also tend to become more secure with their environment, and startle less easily."

Also kn s:
Tennessee Scare Goa
Myotonic Go
Nervous Go
Wooden-Leg Goats
Stiff-Leg Goats

Pictured: Myotonic Goat
This looks embarrassing for the goat

I DEVELOPED A SIMILAR RESPONSE AT SOME POINT WITHOUT EVEN KNOWING IT.

IT IS MOST EASILY IDENTIFIED DURING WHAT IS CALLED "LESBIAN PROCESSING."

I LITERALLY, PHYSICALLY START SHUTTING DOWN.

IT'S BEEN THIS WAY FOR A LONG TIME.

WHAT CAN I SAY? STRESS IS TIRING!
click
Helloooo this is Dr. Laura Schless
NICOLE!
hmm?
How's your food?
?

My Sisters Each Handle Our Mother Differently

She's very sensitive and I love her, but we do have some ground rules.

MEG HAS SET STRICT BOUNDARIES,

I sent the box back unopened.

I can't have someone like that in my life anymore.

AND LIZ HAS CUT HER OUT ENTIRELY.

IT TOOK ME 22 YEARS TO REALIZE I COULDN'T TALK TO HER THE SAME WAY I TALKED TO OTHER PEOPLE. MY JOKES WERE TAKEN TOO PERSONALLY AND TRIGGERED ANGER IN HER THAT I COULDN'T LOGIC MY WAY OUT OF.
DESPITE ALL OF THIS, I STAYED ROOTED, TRYING. I ALREADY HAD AN EMPTY, HOLLOW FEELING WHERE MY FATHER SHOULD HAVE BEEN. I DIDN'T WANT A SEVERED CONNECTION IN THE PLACE OF MY MOTHER, TOO.

Nicole, your mother is a turnip. She's never going to be a sweet potato, no matter what you do or how good you are.

She'll always be a turnip.

Even if I -

Yes, even then.

TO KEEP IN TOUCH AT ALL, I NEEDED TO ACCEPT HER TURNIP STATUS AND WORK AROUND IT, DECIDING WHERE SUCH A ROOT VEGETABLE WOULD AND WOULDN'T FIT IN MY ADULT LIFE.

A typical fight with my Mom
LINENS 'ETC
You still listen to Dr. Laura??
mmm hmm
Oh, she's so mean!
I'M FEELIN' GOOD FROM MY HEAD

Jill! Welcome to the Program
Hi Dr. Laura. I'm calling about my daughter.
So we were talking after the baby shower and it got heated...
...And I said, "You're being a selfish brat."
GASP
Tsk Tsk
What?
I can't believe that woman would call her daughter a selfish brat!
Ha!
???
Mom, you call me a selfish brat all the time!
No I do not.

Nickie, how could you say something like that!?
It is NOT TRUE.
It's TRUE!
Well, here she is, Old Acid Tongue.
but-
You know, you cut me like a knife.
It hurts me, Nickie.
After all that I've done for you.
I flew you here, I gave you a beautiful Christmas!
Anything you want, anything. Oh, Nickie wants this or that, let's go get her her favorite food and make sure princess is happy.

And how do you repay me? You rip me apart!
Well, I'm done. You have no respect. Why don't you just pack up your presents and go back to Portland.
No one can even talk to you. No one but your goofy friends.
Cluck
Soooo Selfish.
Ha. You know what, kid? The world doesn't revolve around you.
You selfish brat.
You don't care about anyone but yourself. You never have.

Help me with these groceries-
-If it's not too much for you, your royal highness.
So what do you want for dinner?
I'd better get started.
Will you let out the guys?
...sure.

BARK!
GRRR
GO, PACO!
C'mere.
You know I love you, sweetheart.
You just make me so mad sometimes! ha ha ha
I know...
Do you need any help?
Grrrr
No, you go rest sweetheart.
Dinner should be ready in an hour.
Come on, boys!
grrrr
BARK!
BARK!

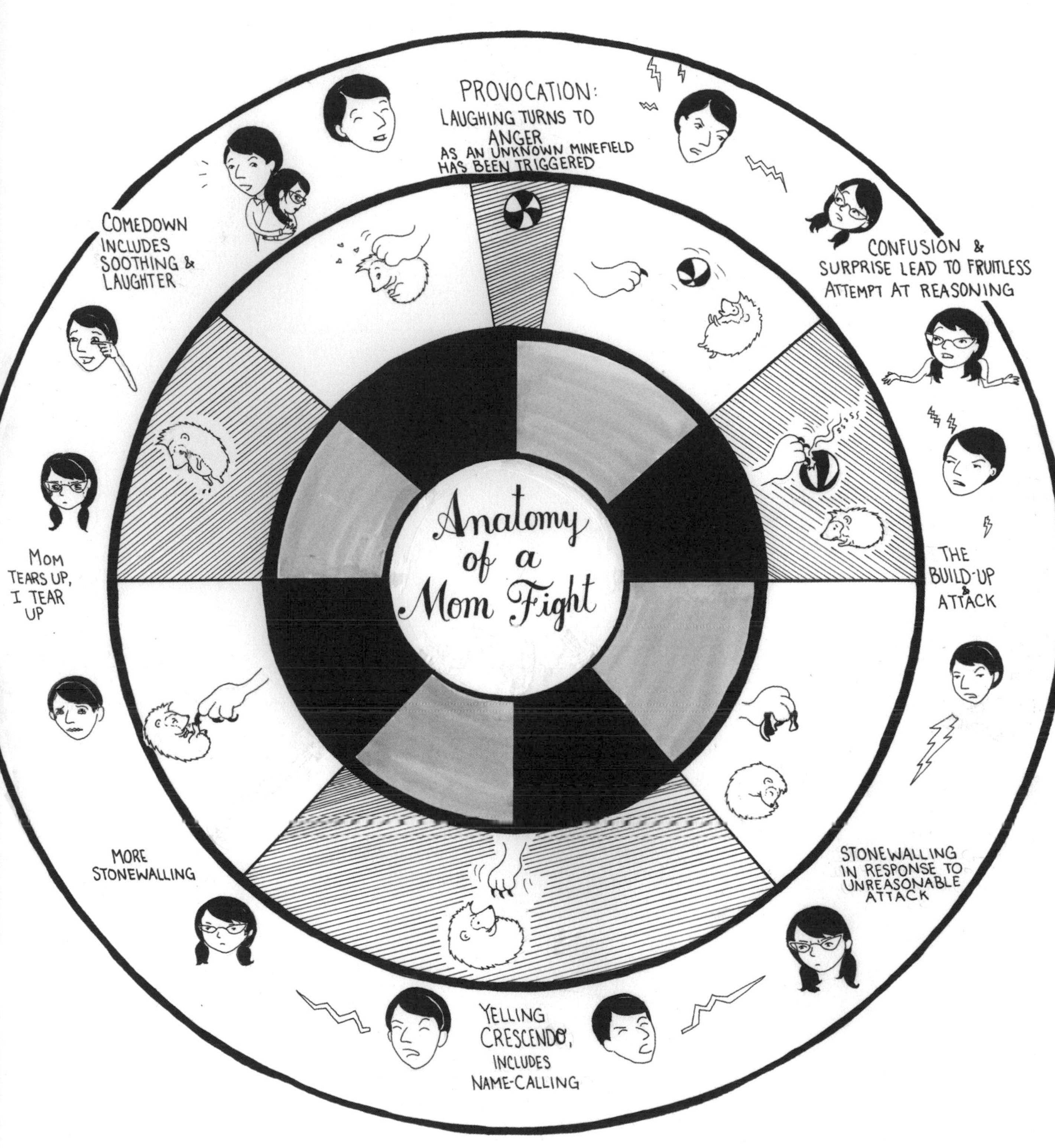
Anatomy of a Mom Fight
PROVOCATION:
LAUGHING TURNS TO ANGER AS AN UNKNOWN MINEFIELD HAS BEEN TRIGGERED
CONFUSION & SURPRISE LEAD TO FRUITLESS ATTEMPT AT REASONING
THE BUILD-UP & ATTACK
STONEWALLING IN RESPONSE TO UNREASONABLE ATTACK
YELLING CRESCENDO, INCLUDES NAME-CALLING
MORE STONEWALLING
MOM TEARS UP, I TEAR UP
COMEDOWN INCLUDES SOOTHING & LAUGHTER

All About Eve
Do you want to go to this party with me?
What's it for again?
It's Eve's breast reduction party. It's your last chance to see her with Gs!
No thanks.
Eve WAS A FRIEND I MADE AT KARAOKE.
SHE ARRIVED IN PORTLAND AFTER DROPPING OUT OF MUSICAL THEATER SCHOOL IN NEW YORK.
I WAS DRAWN IN BY HER AMBITIOUS SONG SELECTIONS (FROM THE SOUND OF MUSIC) AND UNABASHED PAGEANTRY.
Hi!
WHEN RADAR & I MOVED IN TOGETHER, EVE WAS ONE OF MY ONLY FRIENDS WHOM SHE 100% APPROVED OF. VERONA CAUSED JEALOUS TENSION, AND RADAR WASN'T INTERESTED IN HAVING MY GUY FRIENDS AROUND.

These are all my custom bras from age thirteen on-
Wow.
Want one?
No thanks.
I made some vegan cookies you can have.
Oooh.
Hey - I brought you some Tiger Balm.
This WAS MY LAST UNTARNISHED MEMORY OF OUR TIME SPENT AS FRIENDS.
THINGS GOT A LITTLE STICKY BETWEEN US AFTER THIS
Ooooh!
Am I singing flat?
Hmm.
YOU SEE, I STARTED HAVING EVE OVER TO SING WITH ME.
Hey, Nicole, c'mere.
oooOOOoh
I WANTED PROFESSIONAL ADVICE, AND SHE WAS HAPPY TO HELP.

What would you think of Eve guest singing with us?
Totally!
We have a proposition for you-
grr
I WAS RELIEVED TO HAVE A THIRD.
I THOUGHT IT MIGHT CUT THE TENSION BETWEEN RADAR AND ME.
Okay, let's do a high harmony.
oooooh la laaaa la laaAA!
And IT DID- FOR A WHILE...
You're so nice!
Of course!
Radar just grimaces & shakes her head when I sing.
...Before you came along I would cry at practice-
It was like Ike and Tina Turner!
ha ha
Oh, Nicole.

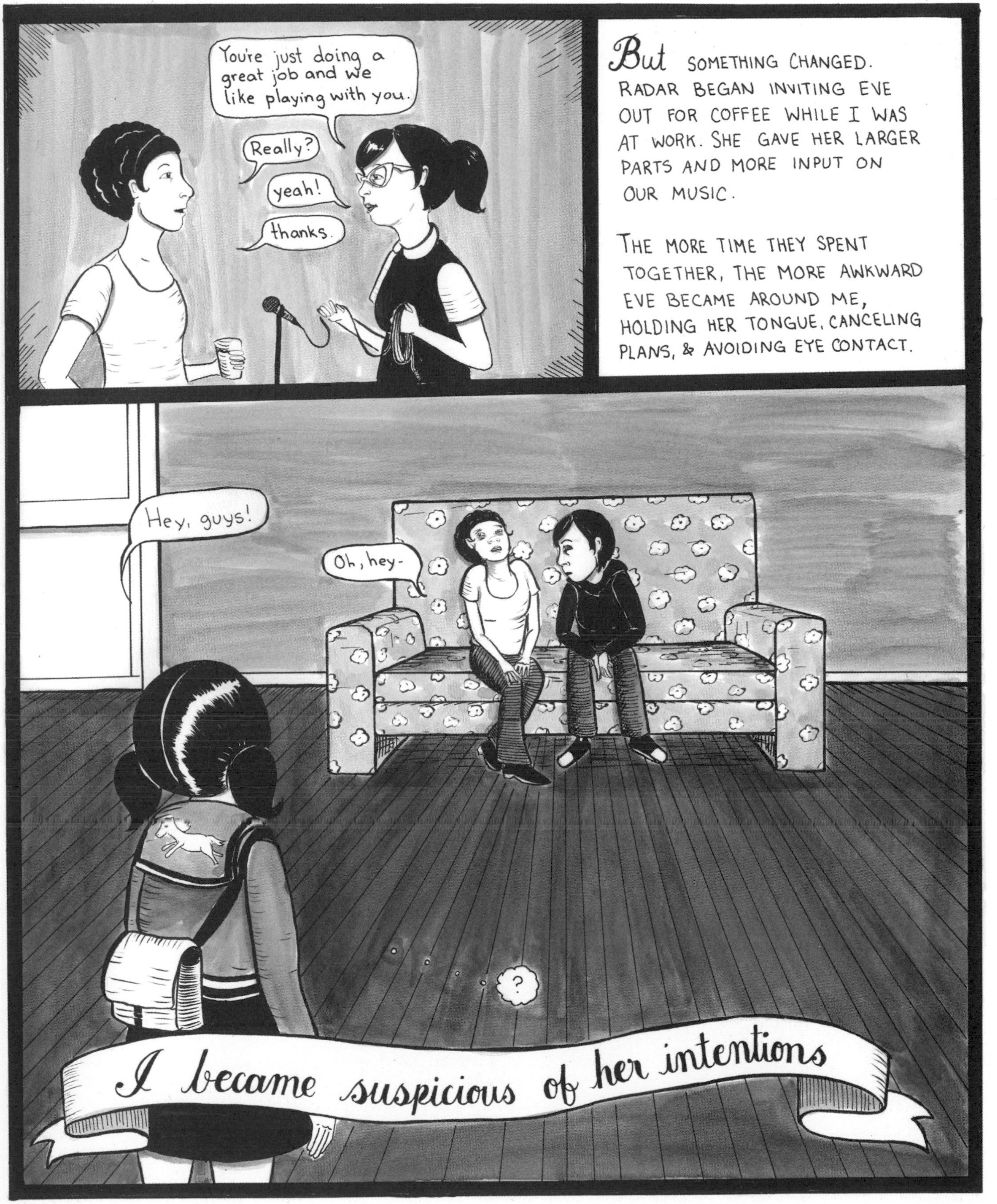

But SOMETHING CHANGED. RADAR BEGAN INVITING EVE OUT FOR COFFEE WHILE I WAS AT WORK. SHE GAVE HER LARGER PARTS AND MORE INPUT ON OUR MUSIC.

THE MORE TIME THEY SPENT TOGETHER, THE MORE AWKWARD EVE BECAME AROUND ME, HOLDING HER TONGUE, CANCELING PLANS, & AVOIDING EYE CONTACT.

Hey, guys!

Oh, hey-

?

I became suspicious of her intentions

IN OTHER WORDS
OPEN♀
MY OTHER CAR IS A BROOMSTICK
WOMEN'S BOOKS & RESOURCES
Hey, Nicole, can you stay late?
Nope- I got a date.
I'm making my mom's Pasta Fagioli recipe for Radar.
oooh.
I'm jealous!
Tell Radar I said hi.
Alberta Grocery
CO-OP
SPECIAL:
99¢/lb
OPEN
golden beets
loose carrots
red cabbage
Heirloom Tomatoes
leek
loose red beets
Fresh Herbs
Green leaf lettuce
ORGANIC Heirloom Tomatoes special! 2.99/lb

Hi, dogs!

Hummm
chop chop chop
Perfect.

Hi, Radar, it's me again
Dinner's ready! Where you at?
I'm starvin'!
Call me!
Hello Hello, Are you okay? Alive?
Maybe you're on the way.
See you soon.
SKRITCH
Hey, Eve, it's Nicole. If you see Radar will you have her call me? I know she may not have reception over there, so thanks in advance. Okay... thank you! Bye!
whine

Hello?
Hey!
You're late.
I am?
I tried to call.
Oh no! I didn't have reception so I turned my phone off.
We were supposed to meet two hours ago.
I was waiting for you.
I'm sorry. Eve really needed my help with this part.
I left her a message, too.
Well, she didn't tell me.
Heyyy...
I can't do this... I can't be with you if you ditch me for other girls. I know she likes you-
It's not like that- Eve & I weren't-
-It doesn't matter, it still just feels bad.
I don't want to be non-monogamous.

Hey. I'm sorry. I'll try to keep an eye on the time, okay?
Forgive me?
Okay.
There is nothing going on with me & Eve, okay?
I know she likes you.
Oh, come on.
She'd never do that.
No?
No!
And anyway, you're the best person I've ever dated, Nicole.
I want to have a family with you!
Don't you want that too?
Yeah.
I do.

I used to tell my Mom everything
Z Z Z Z Z Z Z Z Z Z Z Z Z Z
too hot!
Beija, get down.
I TOLD HER ABOUT MY CREEPY BOYFRIENDS, THE WHOLESOME ONES, EVEN THE PENPALS.
WHEN I WENT GAY, THOUGH, THE INFORMATION CIRCUIT DRIED UP.
Beija takes up the whole bed.
SHE MUST HAVE THOUGHT I WAS GOING THROUGH AN AMAZING DRY SPELL, BECAUSE FOR YEARS I HAD "FRIENDS" INSTEAD OF DATES. BOYFRIENDS TURNED INTO "ROOMMATES."
THERE WERE POINTS WHERE SHE SEEMED TO KNOW,
bzzt bzzt bzzt
Will you turn off my phone?

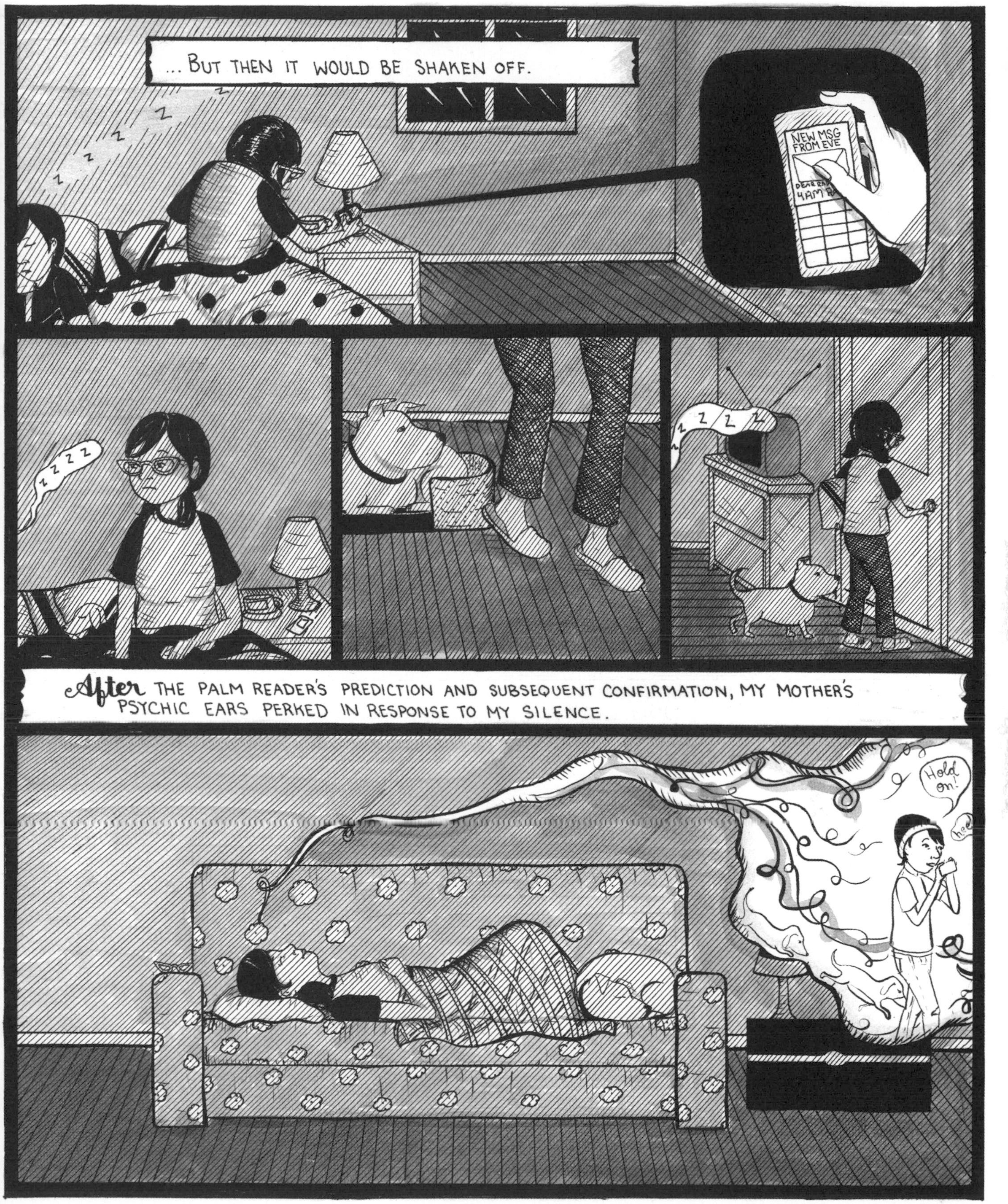

... BUT THEN IT WOULD BE SHAKEN OFF.

NEW MSG FROM EVE

After THE PALM READER'S PREDICTION AND SUBSEQUENT CONFIRMATION, MY MOTHER'S PSYCHIC EARS PERKED IN RESPONSE TO MY SILENCE.

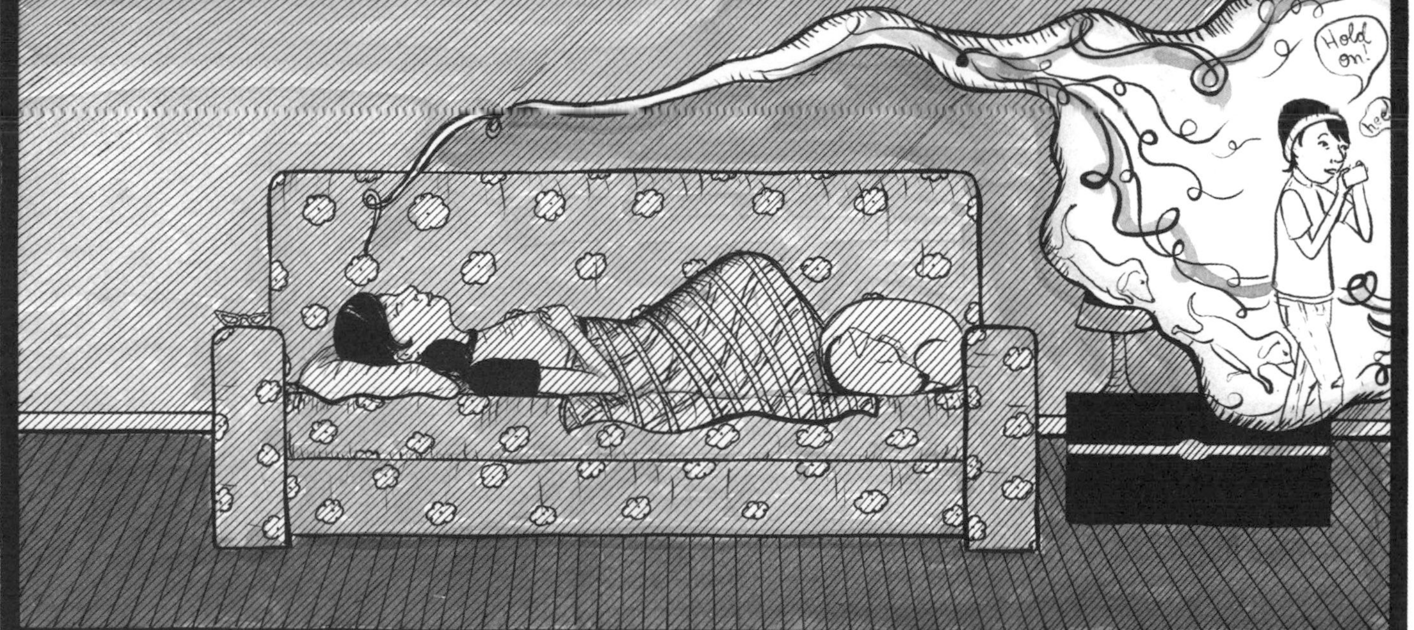

Ahem... Hi guys.
Oh hey.
i should go...
YAWWNN

err-ah-errr!*
*cock-a-doodle-doo
I LEFT GREATER LENGTHS BETWEEN CALLS, EMAILS.
hmm.
brrring!
rrring!
Rrrring!
click
She RESPONDED WITH PERSISTENCE, REACHING FOR A TIGHTER GRASP.
Hi, you've reached Nicole and Radar. We're not here, so please leave a message
Beep!
Nickie, It's your Motherrrr
Let's talk about Christmas!

Let me know, Sweetie, so we can get you a ticket.
CALL YOUR MOTHER! ha ha. Okay. I love you... Call Me! Bye.
I should call her back.
what will yo
BRRRING!
ulp!
Hi, you've reached Nicole & Radar. We're not here, so please leave a message. BEEP
Sorry to call again, but I was just looking through some old photos and I found a great one of you and Tim. Do you have his Mother's address? I'm sure she'd love to have a copy. Bye!
my high school boyfriend

ha ha
Oh my God, she totally has to know we're dating.
Why else would she leave that message?
Wow... what a sneaky lady...
So?
ha ha
What are you going to do?
huh?
About her? I don't know. I have to call her back soon. It's been two weeks!

The only way I'd support you going home is if you said, "I'm gay, who's my dad?"
!!!
Are you serious?
?
hmm.
I gotta go to work.

See you later.
I love you.
bye.
Love you, too.
SLAM

I'm Dr. Laura Schlessinger, proud mother of an American Soldier, .. Hoo-Ah! Becky welcome to
I Love Advice Programs
tell me about it.
wait, wait,
don't tell me.
DEAR ABBY, ANN LANDERS, THEIR HARD-NOSED SUCCESSOR CAROLYN HAX, ASK AMY,
HA!
Ugh. Don't say it, not her.
Don't drive like my brotha!
LOVE LINE, THE TROUBLE SHOOTER TOM MARTINO, CAR TALK, SAVAGE LOVE, AND YES...
...DR. LAURA.

* IT'S WORTH NOTING THAT DR. LAURA HERSELF WAS ONCE A FEMINIST AND LIVED WITH HER CURRENT HUSBAND FOR 8 YEARS BEFORE GETTING MARRIED WHILST PREGNANT. NOT JUDGING, JUST SAYING.

How does she keep her moral edge while being so crude?
If you didn't open your legs this wouldn't have happened.
You're a slave
I'm a slave!
You're a slave
I'm a slave!
You don't want to be a slave, do you?
You want to be a
BRRRING!
hello?
Are you listening to that awful show?
Yes!
She just got some girl to yell "I'm a slave!" before curing her of bulimia...
by telling her to get a job reading to the blind.
Is that even a thing?
I don't think so. I mean, if you were blind would you rather listen to a book on tape in the privacy of your home,
Or have a stuttering college student patronize you?
excuse me, with vomit breath.
You aren't allowed to say that!
Well, I've never heard of that service before.
Hey, I gotta go. The show's back on.
Okay.
Bye.

ONE EIGHT HUNDRED D-R-L-A-U-R-A
Brrring!!
Hi, Nickie, it's your mom again,
Just let me know when to book your flight home. Love you.
hmm
click
I could be an Amber,... a Rose... Theresa?
rrring
rrring

Hello Dr. Laura Show.
My name is Amber Amber Amber Amber Amber Amber Amber Amber Amber
Can I have your name and age, please?
Oh! Nicole - 23
damnit!
Okay, Nicole, are you married?
No.
And how many children?
Zero.
I meant to give them a fake name, but...
And what is your question for Doctor Laura?
What follows is the real life transcript from my call
I TAPED IT.
I'm Doctor Laura Schlessinger, NICOOOLE, Welcome to the program.
Hi, Doctor Laura, thanks for taking my call.
Thank you.
I had a question.
MMM HMM
I found out this year from my sister that my Mom has been lying to me about my father being dead. He's actually alive and -
Slow down. SLOW DOWN.
alright.

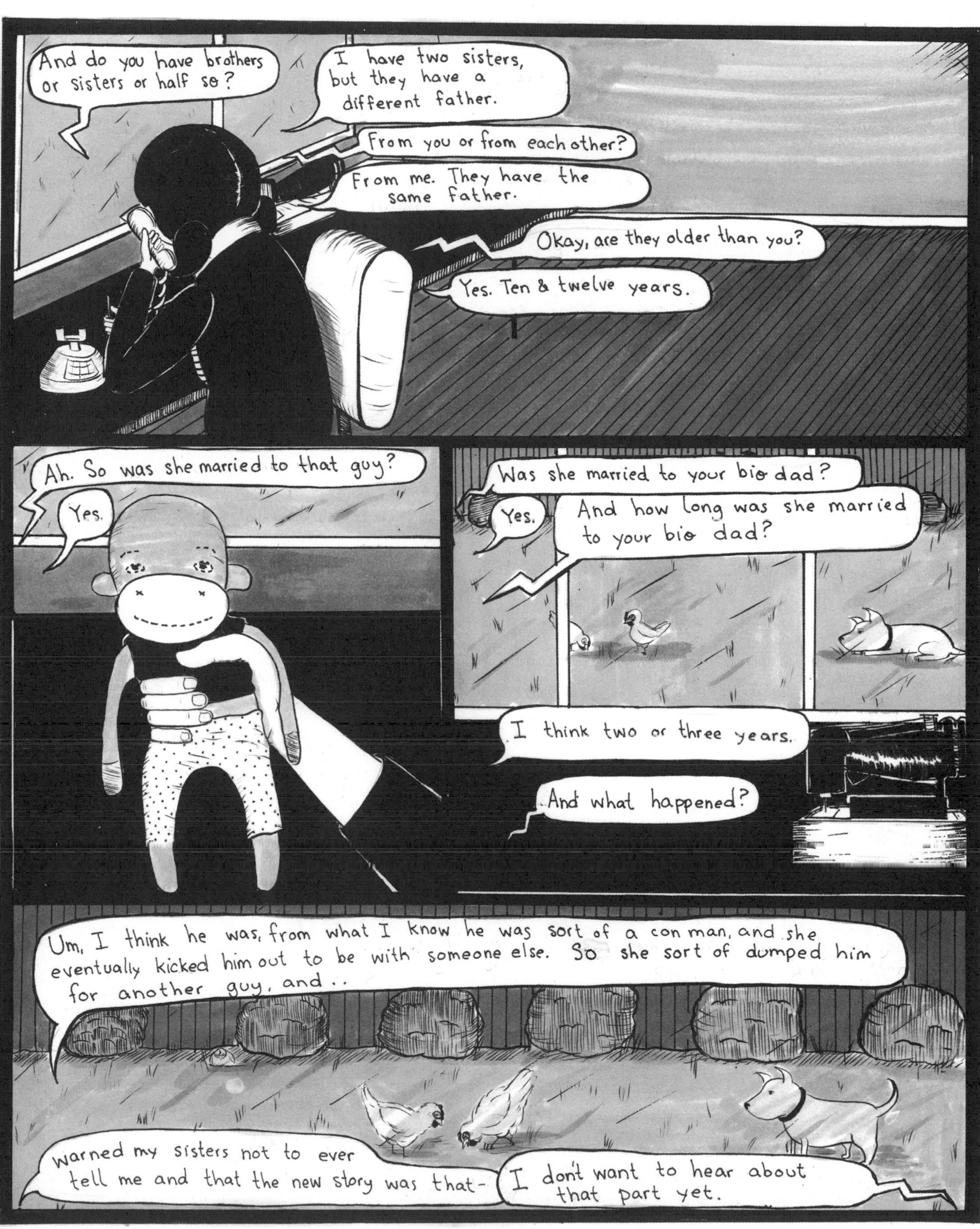
And do you have brothers or sisters or half so?
I have two sisters, but they have a different father.
From you or from each other?
From me. They have the same father.
Okay, are they older than you?
Yes. Ten & twelve years.
Ah. So was she married to that guy?
Yes.
Was she married to your bio dad?
Yes.
And how long was she married to your bio dad?
I think two or three years.
And what happened?
Um, I think he was, from what I know he was sort of a con man, and she eventually kicked him out to be with someone else. So she sort of dumped him for another guy, and..
warned my sisters not to ever tell me and that the new story was that-
I don't want to hear about that part yet.

Okay.
Because I know YOU think that's SO IMPORTANT.
...Okay.
Why, I'll never understand; but okay, So she got rid of the con man.
yeah.
After THIS I RATTED OUT MY MOM FOR SHACKING UP. I SANG LIKE A CANARY, AS I OFTEN DO UNDER PRESSURE. I TURN INTO A COLLANDER FOR ALL THE GRIMACE-INDUCING SECRETS I KNOW. ANYTHING I CAN THINK OF WILL JUST FALL OUT OF MY MOUTH.
You're mad at her, let me ask you another question.
Peck!
When she got rid of your bio-dad, did she move you out of the country, out of the state, out of the city?
No, she-
That's all. So, if anyone knew her at the time they'd know where to find her.
bwaaa
cluck cluck cluck cluck
I think so...
And, well, she didn't move, right, she was in the same town.
yes,
And she didn't throw him out 'til you were two, right?
I think I was one and a half or two, yes.
So no matter what she told anybody she was gonna tell you, he knew you were alive and he didn't even contact you.

Go Ahead. I want to hear the rest of the story now, why you're so mad.
the other small part of him finding me is that she moved out of state a couple years Later, and changed my last name.
Okay, didn't you hear me ask you all those questions?
Um, well-
.. I did, but I was trying to stay in the same year we were talking about, &
I'm not angry with her right now, I'm confused about what I should do.
To summarize the rest of the call...
I TOLD DR. LAURA THE WHOLE STORY. SHE ACTED HOSTILE TOWARD ME & TOLD ME THAT THOUGH MY NAME HAD BEEN CHANGED & I'D BEEN TRANSPORTED TO ANOTHER STATE, MY FATHER COULD STILL FIND ME IF HE WANTED TO, SO I WAS PROBABLY BETTER OFF, AND BASICALLY I SHOULD APPRECIATE THE STABILITY OF MY FAMILY LIFE TODAY INSTEAD OF DREDGING UP THE PAST & FUCKING IT ALL UP. THAT WAS THE GIST.
Did I MENTION THAT I STARTED CRYING LIKE A BABY ABOUT TWO MINUTES INTO THE CALL?
sniff
yeah.
I DID.
You can control how much destruction that (information) will ultimately cause you by how you handle today.
. . . .
That's true. Okay, thanks-
So go have Christmas.
Okay-
You suffered enough. Go have Christmas.
I ALSO KEPT TRYING TO HANG UP WHEN DR. LAURA OFFERED LONG SILENCES IN WHICH TO REFLECT ON THE GRAVITY OF HER WORDS. I'D RUIN THE MOMENT BY BLURTING OUT A "THANKS, DR LAURA" BEFORE BEING SNAPPED BACK INTO SUBMISSION.

NICOLE ON DR. LAURA
hello?
Hi!
SMOOCH
Guess what?
?
I was on the Doctor Laura show today!

?
Why would you call a right-wing conservative talk show therapist about a problem?
...you must be really messed up.
Who's my boy?
How's my queen, Hazel?

Mom Theatre
I can't pay the rent!
You MUST pay the rent.
I CAN'T pay the rent!
You MUST pay the rent.
I'll pay the rent!

My hero!
Bravo!
thank you,
thank you.
ready to go, kiddo?
yes!

COMPARED TO RADAR'S STERN STANCE ON THE SUBJECT, DR. LAURA'S WORDS SEEMED THE EASIEST ON ME.

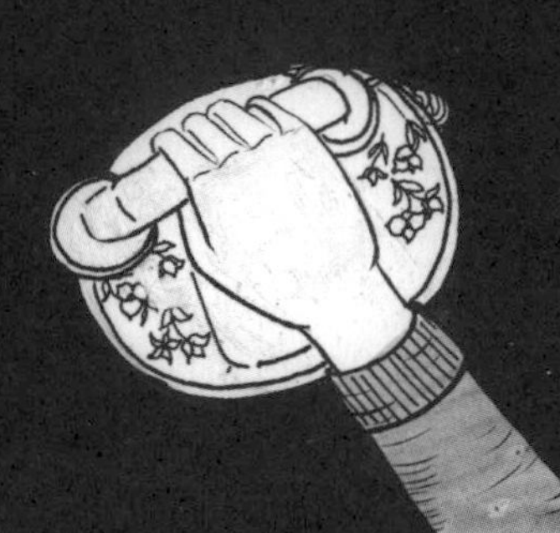

THE PATH OF LEAST RESISTANCE IN A CONFUSING TIME.

My mom's house smells like Yankee Candles.
Banana Nut Muffin Scented Candle
THE CARPET IS BEIGE AND ALWAYS CLEAN.
WHEN I VISIT, SHE CLEANS THE HOUSE FROM TOP TO BOTTOM.
SHE DRESSES HER DOGS IN JINGLE BELL COLLARS AT CHRISTMAS TIME AND CALLS THEM MY "BROTHERS."
SHE SETS UP THE GUEST ROOM,
Franzia
TOFU
AND BUYS VEGAN HEALTH FOOD FOR ME. THINGS LIKE BRAGGS &TOFU THAT WOULD OTHERWISE GO UNTOUCHED IN HER KANSAS REFRIGERATOR.

I COULD FEEL ALL THESE THINGS HAPPENING AS I FOLLOWED THE CONSERVATIVE TALK SHOW HOST'S ADVICE & FLEW HOME TO KANSAS. THE CLEANING & ARRANGING FOR MY VISIT. DOGS GROOMED, TOFU PURCHASED.

MY MOM HAD EXCITED LOVE SHINING OUT OF HER AT THE AIRPORT. SHE ALWAYS WAITS AT THE GATE. I HAD NEVER HAD SO MANY SECRETS & POTENTIAL LIES CHURNING IN MY STOMACH.

YAWWWN
Are you sleepy from your flight?
ahem
Maybe I just need a snack to wake up.
WELCOME TO KANSAS THE SUNFLOWER STATE
I've always said you were my little Narcoleptic.
ha ha, Mom.
yawwn
whirrrr
ha Remember when you got my car stuck on the pole in the garage, Nick? ha ha
You and cars!
sigh.
yep.

You gotta say hi to the guys!
down.
You make yourself at home, honey.
HEY, NICK!
I PUT UP THAT PICTURE YOU SENT ME FROM THE MAGAZINE!
THE ONE OF YOUR BAND!
OH YEAH?
I THOUGHT IT WAS A PHOTO OF YOU & A MAN!
I COULD'VE SWORN IT WAS A MAN, NICK!
MEG AND I HAD TO FIGHT ABOUT IT! SHE SAID, "MOM, THAT'S RADAR, NICKIE'S ROOM-MATE!"
ha...
ha.
gulp
I THINK I'M GOING TO TAKE A NAP, MOM!
OKAY, SWEETIE, I'LL WAKE YOU UP FOR DINNER!

Kansas was tense.
Wait for Grace!
Ooops.
It was not as joyful as Dr. Laura had imagined.
Please bless these gifts we are about to receive, and thank you for bringing Nickie here safely to our home.
The stress of keeping the secrets kept a migraine pressure on my skull.
Amen.
It left me seeming distant and closed off, unable to enjoy any of the moments I was offered.

Father
son
A-hem
Holy Spirit.
Amen.
Hi, it's me. Just calling to say hi.
Call me when you get home. ...I love you.
I BODE MY TIME ON THE COUCH.
NOT BEING GAY.
HAVING A DEAD FATHER.
Good sauce, hon.
I NEEDED A LITTLE RELIEF.
So Nickie's seeing her buddy tonight.
Yeah. I'm sleeping over at D's house.

Well, call when you get in, Honey.
I will!
May I be excused?
Go on.
Remember this one, 'the Booty Crank'?!?
ha!
???
I do!
I'm all wound up!
I've been watching t.v. all day for a week!
Do you guys want to get fries after this?

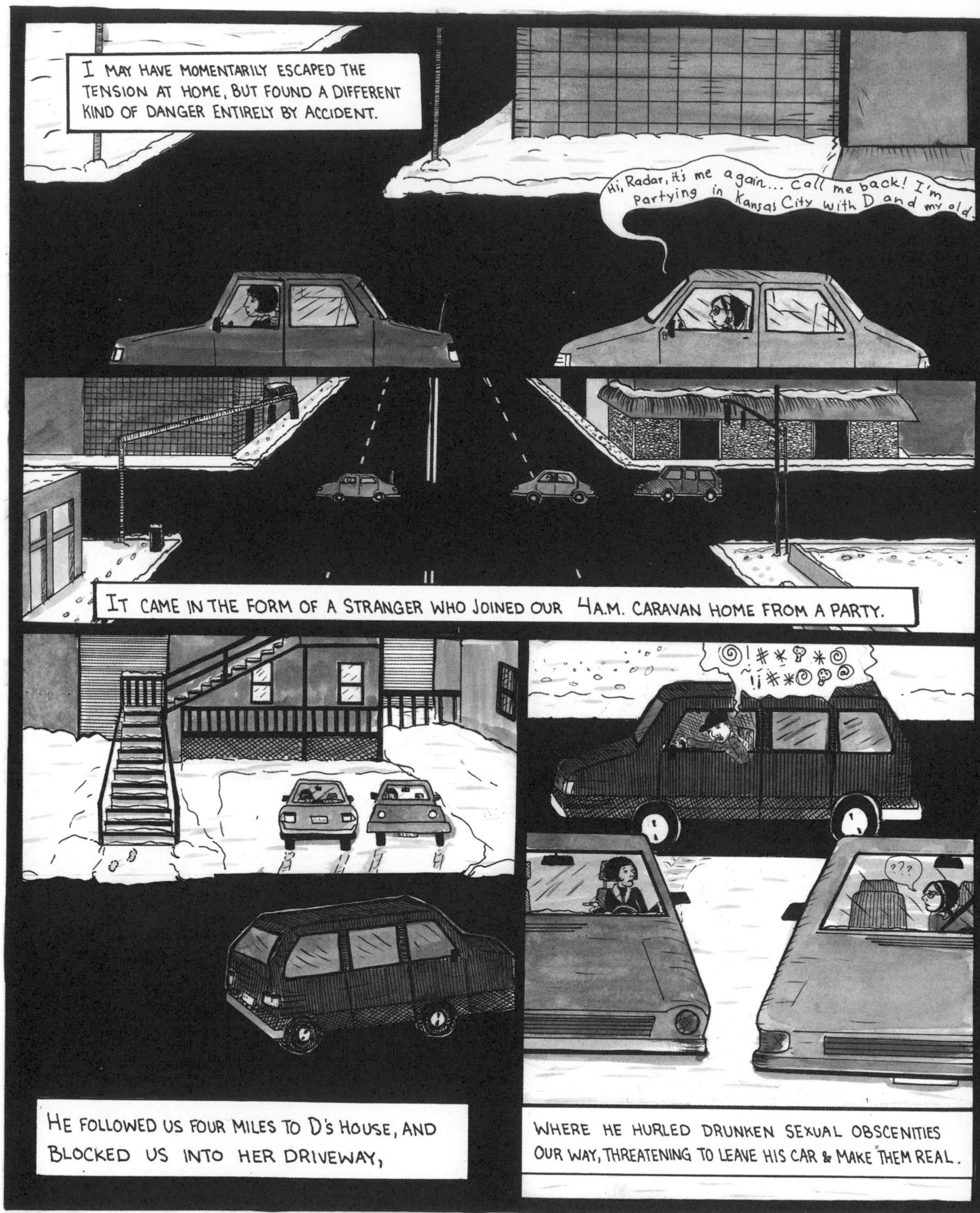
I MAY HAVE MOMENTARILY ESCAPED THE TENSION AT HOME, BUT FOUND A DIFFERENT KIND OF DANGER ENTIRELY BY ACCIDENT.
Hi, Radar, it's me again... Call me back! I'm partying in Kansas City with D and my old.
IT CAME IN THE FORM OF A STRANGER WHO JOINED OUR 4A.M. CARAVAN HOME FROM A PARTY.
???
HE FOLLOWED US FOUR MILES TO D's HOUSE, AND BLOCKED US INTO HER DRIVEWAY,
WHERE HE HURLED DRUNKEN SEXUAL OBSCENITIES OUR WAY, THREATENING TO LEAVE HIS CAR & MAKE THEM REAL.

9-1-1
Hi, there's a stranger blocking me into my drive way + screaming.
THERE WAS REALLY NOWHERE TO GO.
I CALLED 9-1-1!
father, son, holy spirit, amen
screeee!
IN COMPARISON, THE DANGER AT MOM'S WASN'T SO GREAT.
That was awful! Who was that???
I think I'm going back to sleep at my Mom's house....
FOR ONE NIGHT I COULD APPRECIATE THE SAFETY THAT SHE WAS TRYING SO HARD TO OFFER.

I almost got killed!
He could've done anything - We were trapped!
You were out until 4 A.M.?
Nicole, it's your own fault.
...
Why would you do this to yourself?
We were just coming home, I didn't -
No. Not that.
I mean your trip to Kansas. To your mother.

Did you tell her?
No.
So you stayed at these people's house the whole time and didn't tell them?
yes.
And you acted straight.
I can't talk to you right now.
When you're making choices to hurt yourself like this.
It wasn't that big of a deal...
It's my family.
I've got to go to band practice anyway.
Sniff.
arf! arf!
arf!
arf!
sniff

Hi, dogs.
Looks like your mom put up the Christmas lights, Lou.
Welcome home, Nicole. We missed you.

KNOCK
KNOCK
rruff
hi.
hi
I made nachos. You want some?

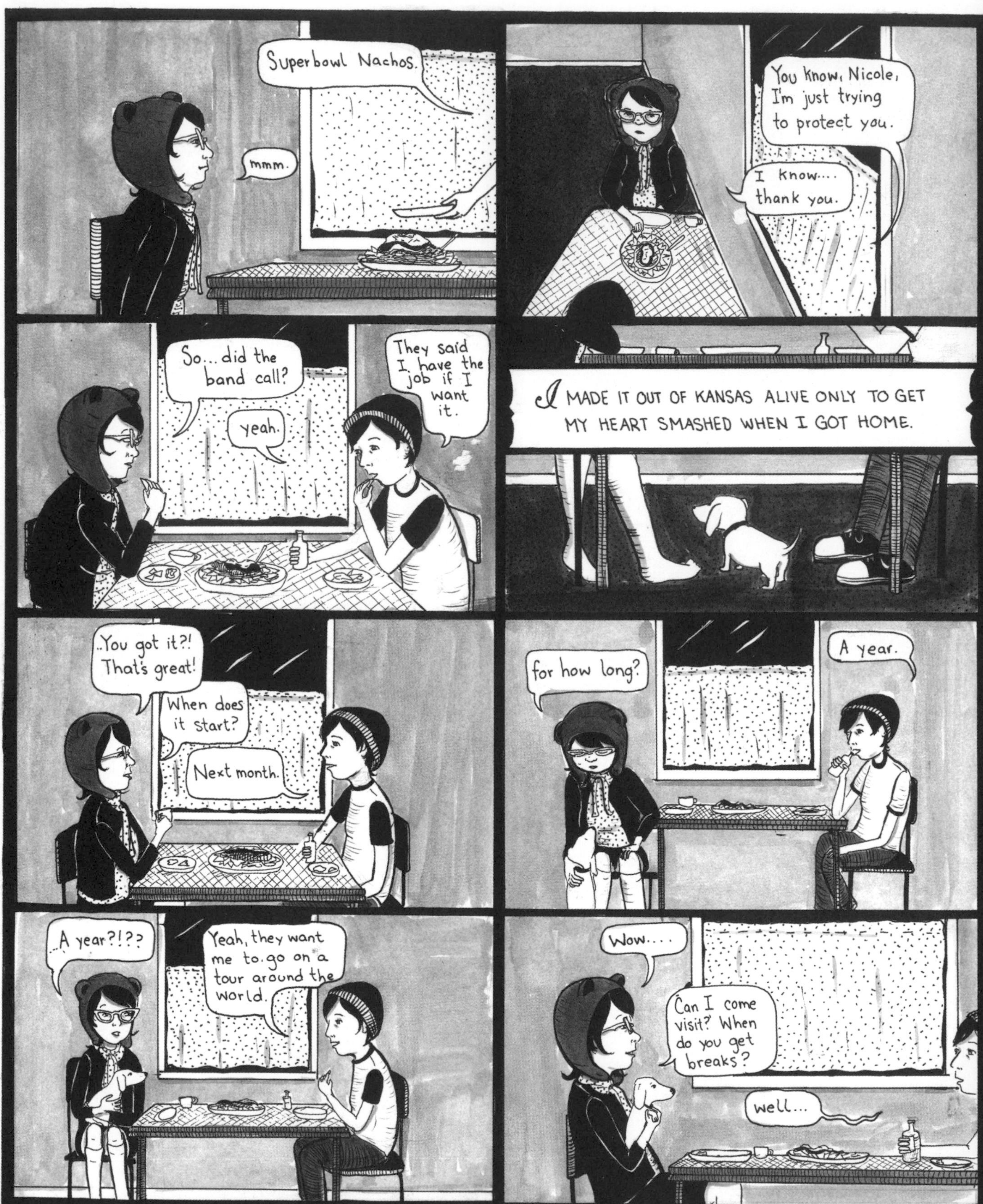
Superbowl Nachos.
mmm.
You know, Nicole, I'm just trying to protect you.
I know.... thank you.
So... did the band call?
yeah.
They said I have the job if I want it.
I MADE IT OUT OF KANSAS ALIVE ONLY TO GET MY HEART SMASHED WHEN I GOT HOME.
..You got it?! That's great!
When does it start?
Next month.
for how long?
A year.
..A year?!??
Yeah, they want me to go on a tour around the world.
Wow....
Can I come visit? When do you get breaks?
well...

Things HADN'T BEEN GOING WELL. THAT PART OF RADAR'S STATEMENT WAS TRUE.

I'D BEEN GOING CRAZY LATELY. THE MORE TIME RADAR AND EVE SPENT TOGETHER, THE MORE INSECURE I FELT, AND MY INSECURITY WAS MANIFESTING INTO IRRATIONAL FEARS FOR MY PHYSICAL SAFETY IN OUR EMPTY HOUSE.

I CLUNG TO RADAR FIERCELY, ANGRY THAT SHE LEFT ME AT HOME TO GET ROBBED OR MURDERED WHILE SHE CAROUSED WITH A GIRL WHO MOST CERTAINLY HAD A CRUSH ON HER. RADAR CALLED ME CRAZY, PARANOID, JEALOUS & WRONG. SHE STAYED OUT LONGER EACH NIGHT.

The disparity between my perception & Radar's words chipped away at my brain until I was one giant exposed nerve, primal & neurotic.
BRRRING!
Trust Trust Trust Trust
hello?
Nicole! I wasn't AVOIDING you, we were just out smoking!
sorry.
Look, we're really jamming here. I probably won't be home 'til 2 A.M.
okay. bye.
Maybe it was best to end things; but I wondered -
What about our band?
umm..
I don't want to play music with you anymore.
What?
Just like that? No conversation or anything?
yeah..
Look, I was going to do it in a letter, but I decided to tell you in person.
bravo.

What about Eve?
She and I will still play together.
..But not as this band?
That's not yours to say.
It's a two person band, what do you mean it's not mine to say?
It's my band.
Did she know before now?
yes.
And we're still playing a show before I leave town. She'll be singing your parts and playing the drums.
What is going on?
How could I not see it?

I TOLD You MY fear of being Replaced
I'm not replacing you.
Then what are you doing?
Playing music with someone else instead.
Why does it have to be her?
I just dedicated a year of hard work to this & there's no conversation? Nothing?
I'm going to stay at Eve's for a while.
I HAD UNWITTINGLY CREATED A FAMILY NO MORE STABLE THAN THE ONE I GREW UP WITH. I BASED A WHOLE RELATIONSHIP ON THE ILLUSION OF SECURITY & MANUFACTURED SAMENESS.

rrring
rrring
rrring
rrrring!
rrring

Ack
rrring
click.
Hi, you've reached
Nicole and Rada
We're not here s
please leave a-
Nicole, are you there? Pick up.....
Pick up the phone if you're there.... Ah,
anyway, it's Radar. Eve and I are coming
to pick up Lou later to take him to
his new home. Please get his stuff
ready. Okay..... bye.

click.
AAAH!
Fuck
You
Fuck you
Fuck you
Fuck you!
I Hate you!

You're making me do this.
No I'm not!
I can't watch four dogs for a YEAR!
two is a lot!
Then I have no choice.
What about Lamb?
I think Eve's room-mates will take Lamb-Chop.
But he's twelve! You can't just get rid of him.
Well??
What am I supposed to do?
Give me Lambchop. I'll take him.
He deserves a home he's familiar with.
Ugh, fine.
-but you won't take Lou?
I'm already watching two of your dogs while you're gone - I can't take all four.
FINE. Then I guess I have to give him away. It's your choice.

C'mon Lou!
Loooouu!
Vrrooo m
Lamb

Q & A with Nicole G.
re: This whole Dad thing
1. What happened when you asked your extended family about your Dad? Surely SOMEONE must remember him!
You would think so, right?
Never underestimate the secret-keeping skills of the Georges family, dear reader.
Here is an example of what happened.
Hi, Uncle Wally!
I got your email, sweetheart. Why did you refer to yourself as estranged? Honey, we're your family.
yeah...
Sorry, Uncle Wally, it was supposed to be a joke....
Well any way, to answer your question, I don't know who your father was.
Oh, really? Hmm... Meg & Liz said you were friends with him at the time...
Well, your sisters must be mistaken. I don't know who your father is.
Oh.
But your mother's really gotten her life together since then.

She's so active in her church, and she's got Pete, It's a blessing, Nickie.
Yeah... yeah, it's great! Okay, bye, Uncle Wally.
Bye, sweetheart. You call anytime! Your family loves you.
QUESTION #2. Why not just ask your mom right away?
Ha!
That's a good one!
But seriously, what good could come from asking my Mom? She kept this a secret for 23 years. I didn't expect her to say "Phew! You got me!!"
Knowing Sabine like I do, I knew she'd just defend herself-
And somehow turn it around so that somehow she was the victim here.
Don't ask me how she'd do it. it's secret Mom Magic.
Not the solace & comfort I was seeking, you know?

#3. Why didn't you find your dad right away?
Good question.
To understand my decision you need to step inside my brain & understand two very influential factors:
My idea of fathers in general,
and my idea of my own father.
I grew up with a cast of characters, all charged with the role of Dad.
I was made to call Ed "Daddy."
aroma de Asshole
Ed, who smoked indoors, stuck in his La-Z-Boy watching Jeopardy when he wasn't calling my teen sister a 'bitch' or beating my mom.
Next in line was Pete, who was a stand-up guy in comparison, but who was mostly there for Mom romance, and got in on the Father game a little too late.
I was a jaded, angry 11 year old who didn't see the need for a Dad & treated Pete with indifference - just an obstacle between me & my mother.
Let us not even mention Faisal, the Arab prince who was first in line for fatherhood post-David, & who quickly bolted.
gulp
fatherhood?

I saw the value of fathers only a few times
PRIDE
When men gave away the bride at weddings
I'm leaving my safe, stable home for a new one.
and then tearfully shared the first dance
Nice to MEET YOU
Don't try anything
Or when Pete would crush the hands of potential suitors as I grew older.
A protector and admirer.
As for my own father, I thought he was a con man who didn't want to be found.
My daughter! I've been looking for you my whole life!
Oh, Daddy!
Finally, we are a family, just like I've always dreamt of.
bzzz!
If I did find a 60 year old ex-con and come out of the wood-work as his long-lost daughter, what could I expect?
Call me a pessimist, but it didn't sound like meeting David would be a warm & fuzzy heartfelt reunion. I imagined it would be an awkward meeting. More of a...
I don't have any money, if that's what you're after.
Nope, I just wanted to meet. Here I am, your long lost lesbian cartoonist daughter.
Hmm.
Wait - do you have any money?
uhh...
I was skeptical, so I hung back, instead building a family with my surly sweetheart & living in a lush landscape of gays, artists, and dogs.

I hope this clears some things up, folks.
This concludes the Dad edition of Q&A with Nicole G.
Now back to our story.

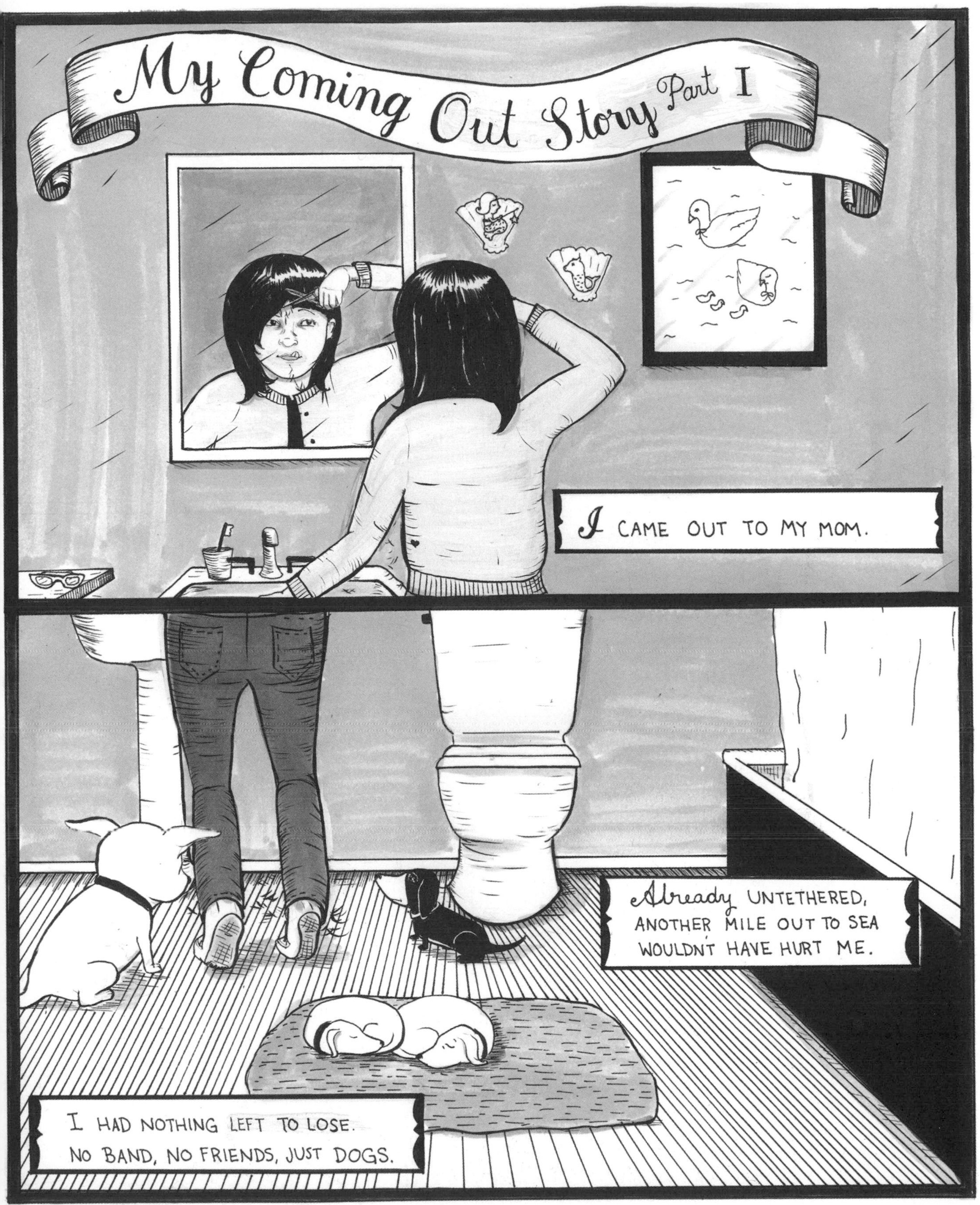
My Coming Out Story Part I
I CAME OUT TO MY MOM.
Already UNTETHERED, ANOTHER MILE OUT TO SEA WOULDN'T HAVE HURT ME.
I HAD NOTHING LEFT TO LOSE. NO BAND, NO FRIENDS, JUST DOGS.

My mom called & called. She wanted to visit.
I'm sure her psychic antennae were going crazy after my breakup.

SHE WAS PUSHING SO HARD, I BROKE.
Watch out, Lamb,
Needles are sharp!
I BROKE AND THE TRUTH CAME OUT.

FR: NJG@Meowface.com
To: KSCATHOLIC@AOL.COM

Dear Mom,

I'm gay, who's my Dad?

NOT IN SO MANY WORDS,

Dear Mom,
Hi. How are you?

I wanted to write (before you bought your ticket to Portland) to clear up a couple of things.

IN PARTICULAR, SOME UNTRUTHS.

I FOLLOWED RADAR'S ADVICE.

BUT THAT WAS THE GIST.

Firstly, Radar and I were not roommates or best friends.
We were in love, and now we're not.
It's been really hard on me.
I'm still taking care of her dogs while she's away. They're really nice dogs, Mom, & they've been keeping me company when I get sad here.

I want to apologize for lying to you, but I know you've been dishonest about something too, and my hope is that we can clear everything up at once.

I know that my Dad is alive.

I found out on my own, then had it confirmed by Meg & Liz.
Nobody came to me about it.
I'm not sure what to say, but as of now I'm not angry & we don't have to go into it via email.

Anyway, I still love you & I wanted to give you the chance to have all the facts before you bought a ticket to visit. Here's to honesty, N.G.

A DOUBLE HITTER, JUST TO CLEAR THE AIR.

SHE DIDN'T PUMMEL ME WITH SLANDERS LIKE SHE DID LIZ.
IN FACT, SHE DIDN'T RESPOND AT ALL.

NOT FOR THREE DAYS, THAT IS. CHATTERBOX MOM, LOVER OF DAILY CALLS & INBOX ASSAULTS, WAS SILENT.

WHEN SHE DID RESPOND IT WAS CIVIL. UNDERSTATED. I IMAGINED EMAIL WAS WORKING AS A DAM BETWEEN ME & HER AUTHENTIC REACTION. WE EXCHANGED TENSE PLEASANTRIES ONLINE AS I NERVOUSLY PREPARED FOR HER ARRIVAL IN PORTLAND. I WAS READY FOR THE WORST.

My Coming Out Story, Part II: Mom's Visit
NEWSPAPERS
Nickie!
Hi, sweetheart! Look at how long your hair is!
Let's see - you got any more tattoos?
ha ha
Mom-

So where are you taking me first?
I've got to freshen up.
I'm staying in that great B and B I found-
I thought we could stop by my house-
What a funny little car!
I like that it's so solid.
Well, good, it'll keep you safe, honey.
bark! bark bark!!
arf! bark!
Oh, what a sweet house.
Oh, they're so cute!
Do you still have those chickens? ha ha
Yeah... but the dogs chase them, so mostly they stay in the coop.
Nickie and her menagerie, ha ha
...And this is where I draw and sew-
Oh how nice.
TELL THAT TRIFLIN BITCH SHE CAN HAVE

Have a seat, Nick. Let's visit.
So, I got your email...
When I read it I cried for three days straight.
Three days and three nights.
Oh. You did?
Pete wanted to take me to the hospital, I couldn't stop crying.
Really?!?
I was just so upset.
Sniff
But I talked to a Christian counselor, a priest, and he made me feel a lot better.
He calmed me down.
He assured me I won't go to hell for raising two lesbians.
It really eased my mind.

But Nickie- A Lesbian?
How can you be a lesbian?
Didn't you like making love to men?
Ugh - Mom!
Well!
Are you telling me you like making love to a woman more than making love to a man?
Mom!
I don't want to talk about "Making Love"!
Why not!?!
Are you a prude, Nickie? Is that what you are?
Ech! No!
I just don't want to talk about it.

Okay, you know what?
If you wanna be a lesbian, be a lesbian.
Ha Ha
I'm 60 years old, I'm too old for this shit.
Ha Ha
Wow. ..Ha ha..
Okay... hmm!
Ahem.
So... you know about David?
Yawwwn
Yeah.
...Who told you?
No one. I found out from a psychic!
You did? No kidding!
Ha.
Well, it figures David would get busted by a palm reader- he was so psychic.

Really?
Oh yeah. And he was brilliant. So sharp- just like you...
...but he was a bad guy.
I just didn't tell you because I didn't want you to feel abandoned.
He left us.
He didn't want you.
So you see, Nickie, I was protecting you!
Mmm Hmm

Shiver
Anyway, it's over. He's gone.
Where are we going?
I guess we should check into your B & B.
Great! I'll get my coat.

He's a good dog.
So old!

So you really don't like making love to men?
Mom! Ew!

That was it.
THE ANTICLIMAX OF MY WHOLE PARENTED LIFE.
MOM REACTED AS EXPECTED. SHE KICKED HER MISTAKE UNDER THE COUCH & KEPT MOVING.
IF I WANTED TO KEEP A PARENT, I NEEDED TO FORGIVE AND ACCEPT HER AS SHE WAS-
A 60 YEAR OLD WOMAN WITH AN ENORMOUS CAPACITY TO LOVE IN THE PRESENT;
BUT NEVER RECONCILE THE PAST.
I CUT MY LOSSES AND MOVED FORWARD.

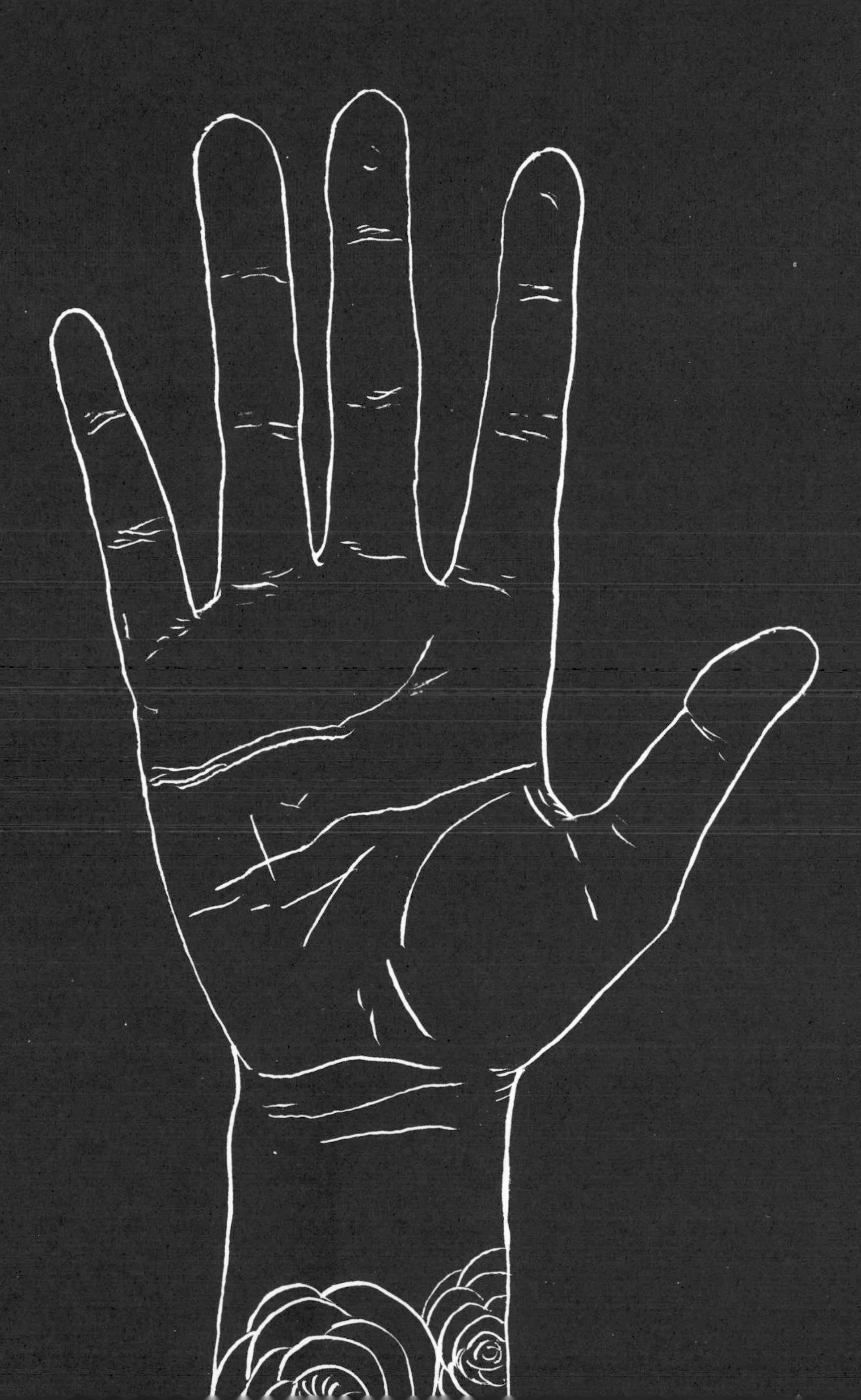

EPILOGUE
FIVE YEARS FROM THAT TALK FOUND ME WORKING ON THIS BOOK FROM A DESK IN MY OWN LITTLE HOUSE, JUST TEN BLOCKS FROM THE GINGERBREAD MANOR WHERE THIS STORY BEGAN.
Hey Beija,
Come inside!
NO SOLICITORS Thank You

EVERYONE WHO HEARD THE STORY- ABOUT MY FAMILY, MY DAD & DR. LAURA- ASKED THE NATURAL QUESTION:

THE TRUTH IS, I HADN'T.

I TRIED ONCE, RIGHT AFTER THE MOM CHAT,

BUT HAD COME TO A DEAD END BASED ON THE COMMON-NESS OF HIS NAME, & MY UNWILLINGNESS TO PUSH THROUGH THE BARRIER BY PLUGGING MONEY INTO A DETECTIVE WEBSITE.

MY EMOTIONAL RESERVES AT THAT POINT WEREN'T ROBUST ENOUGH TO HANDLE A MEETING, HIS POSSIBLE INMATE STATUS, OR A DENIAL OF PATERNITY.

I ABANDONED THE SEARCH, JUST AS MOM SAID HE'D ABANDONED ME.

As I was finishing this book, covered in ink and steeped in familial thought, I decided to try one more time.
I told myself it was just for the book. Just for art's sake.
R.I.P.
Sir LAMBCHOP
tap tap tap tap
I visited the usual people-finding websites,
tap
tap
tap
Only this time I took out my credit card and held my breath.

I USED WHAT I KNEW ABOUT SOCIAL NETWORKING TO LOOK UP DAVID'S SONS.

IT WASN'T HARD THIS TIME. THEIR NAMES APPEARED RIGHT AWAY, CONNECTED TO EACH OTHER.

This is going to sound weird, but I am almost 100% positive we are related, and we share the same father, that person being David Denmark.
I am the daughter he had with a woman named Sabine.
My family told me David was dead(!) for most of my life, and only about six years ago did I discover the truth.
Anyway, I am only writing to say hello and get in touch.
If you are interested in emailing at all, I am very curious to hear any information about him or yourselves that you may have. If this all sounds totally bizarre and you'd rather not be in touch, I understand.
Sincerely, Nicole

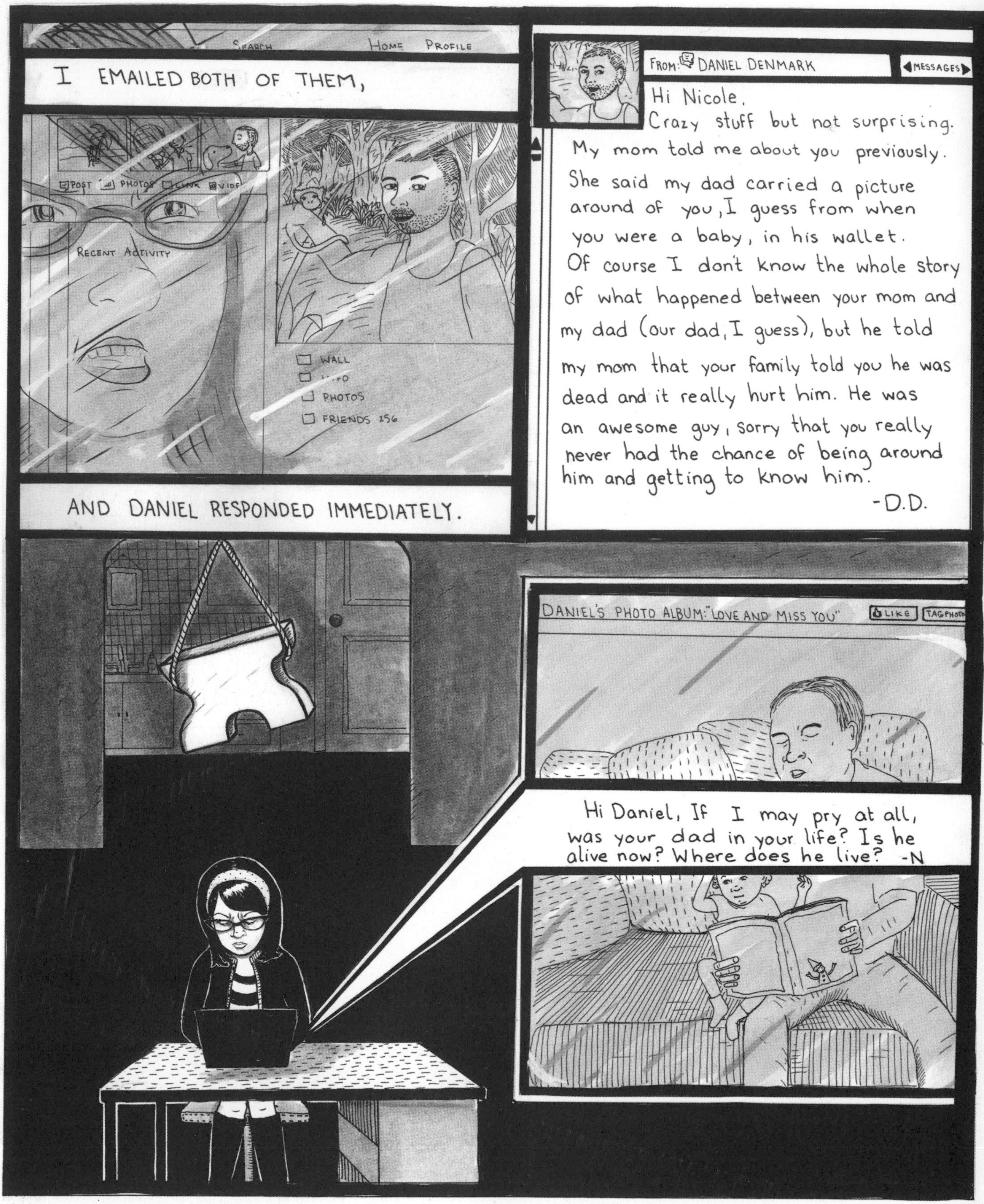

SEARCH HOME PROFILE

I EMAILED BOTH OF THEM,

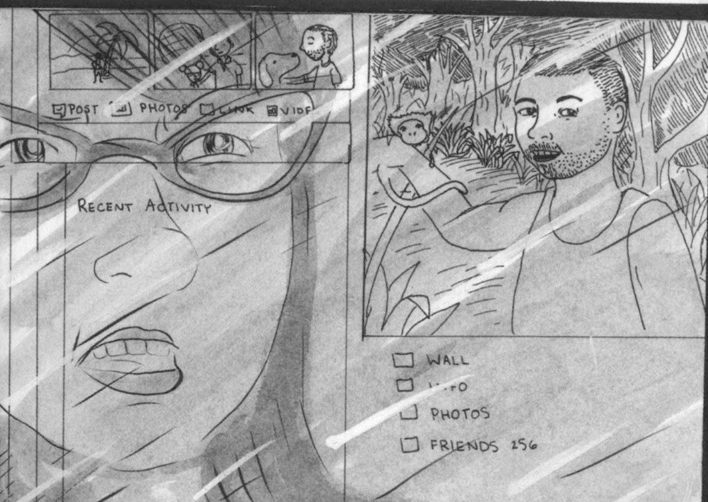

AND DANIEL RESPONDED IMMEDIATELY.

FROM: DANIEL DENMARK

MESSAGES

Hi Nicole,
Crazy stuff but not surprising.
My mom told me about you previously.
She said my dad carried a picture around of you, I guess from when you were a baby, in his wallet.
Of course I don't know the whole story of what happened between your mom and my dad (our dad, I guess), but he told my mom that your family told you he was dead and it really hurt him. He was an awesome guy, sorry that you really never had the chance of being around him and getting to know him.
-D.D.

DANIEL'S PHOTO ALBUM: "LOVE AND MISS YOU"

LIKE

TAG PHOTO

Hi Daniel, If I may pry at all, was your dad in your life? Is he alive now? Where does he live? -N

Yes, he was in my life. Sadly he passed away in August of 2009, of heart complications.

10000 LBS

He was awesome and I miss him every day.

Also, you look just like him! Have you seen pictures of him at all?

I'm really sorry that he was made up to be some type of con guy. It's honestly 100% not him. He was a football coach & things like that, lol.

You will see a lot of yourself in his pictures. He was definitely a creative guy, a lot like yourself. He was always building things & had like 10 patents of all types. He was really smart.

Dear Daniel,

Thank you so much for taking time to tell me about your dad. I truly appreciate it.

The whole story is sad & is blowing my mind. I'm really sorry you lost him so soon. 61 is too young.

-N.

Nicole,
My dad is also your dad! There is a lot you can learn about him, and I think it would really help out.

It was definitely too young to lose him.

-Daniel

DENMARK
DAVID DANIEL
MM3 USN
VIETNAM
1948 - 2009
GONE BUT NOT FORGOTTEN

THANK YOU

To everyone who helped create this book:

Holly Bemiss -- A champion without whom this story would exist only as a series of cryptic 'zine pages, and who has faithfully and patiently supported *Calling Dr. Laura* for the past five years.
Meagan Stacey and Johnathan Wilber -- For helping this book reach its full potential through keen eyes and thoughtful editing.
My readers and advisers Aaron Renier, Chelsey Johnson, & Hope Hitchcock.
Time-Management Coach Alec Longstreth.
Christopher Moisan, Beth Fuller, Katrina Kruse, & everyone at HMH.

This 100% Could Not Exist without technology wizard Harlan Mahaffy, whose contribution over the past four years is so extreme that I think I might owe him an organ.

Michelle Tea -- for supporting this book and the proposed title *Nicole Georges & the Sorcerer's Stone*, and for taking this story across the country via Sister Spit.
Thank you also to RADAR Productions (including Michelle Tea, Beth Pickens & Ali Liebegott),
for giving me space at your Lab to work in peace.
Thank you to the Janowski Family for the use of their cabin retreat.

Katy Davidson, who is very patient.

My sister Meg. My sister Liz, who is the first artist I ever admired.
Ilvs, Greig Means, Alison Bechdel, sts,
Mary Beth Ditto, Jae Choi,
Sarah Dougher, Marc Parker, Dylan Williams, Nate Backous.
The IPRC, Carolyn Berk & Lovers.

Radar Von Krone, thank you for pushing me towards the truth that drastically changed my life,
and David for being so generous, open and kind.

Lastly, thank you to my mom.